NUTSHELLS

English Legal System

NINTH EDITION

by
Professor PENNY DARBYSHIRE
Kingston University

SWEET & MAXWELL
THOMSON REUTERS

First Edition – 1989
Second Edition – 1992
Third Edition – 1995
Fourth Edition – 1998
Fifth Edition – 2001
Sixth Edition – 2004
Seventh Edition – 2007
Eighth Edition – 2010

Published in 2013 by Thomson Reuters (Professional) Limited
(Registered in England & Wales, Company No 1679046.
Registered Office and address for service:
100 Avenue Road, London NW3 3PF)
trading as Sweet & Maxwell

**For further information on our products and services, visit www.sweetandmaxwell.co.uk*

Typeset by YHT Ltd, London
Printed in Great Britain by Ashford Colour Press, Gosport, Hants

No natural forests were destroyed to make this product; only farmed timber was used and re-planted

A CIP catalogue record for this book is available from the British Library.

ISBN: 978-0-414-02643-8

Contents

Using this Book

DETAILED TABLE OF CONTENTS for easy navigation.

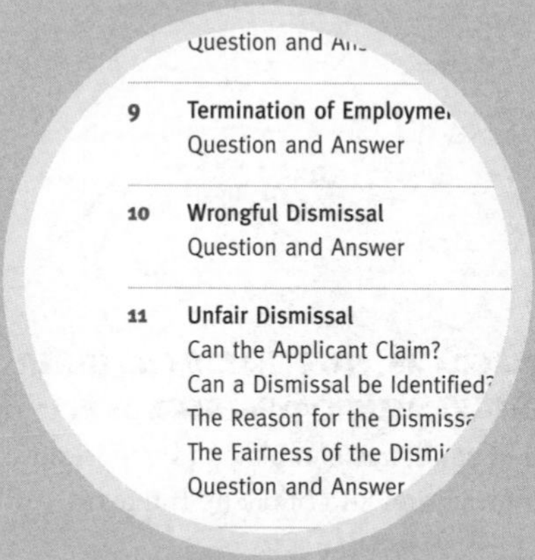

TABLES OF CASES AND LEGISLATION for easy reference.

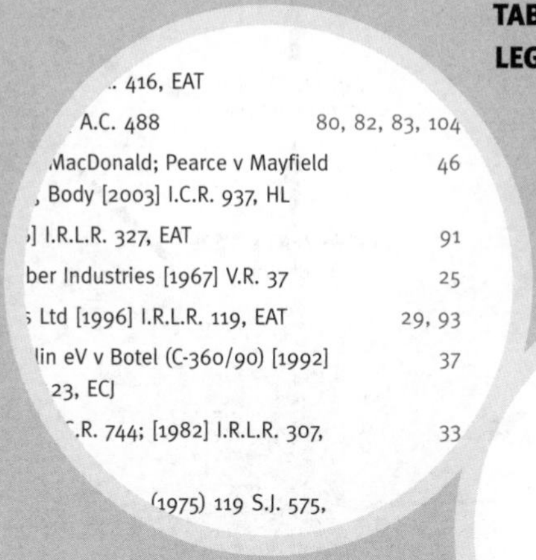

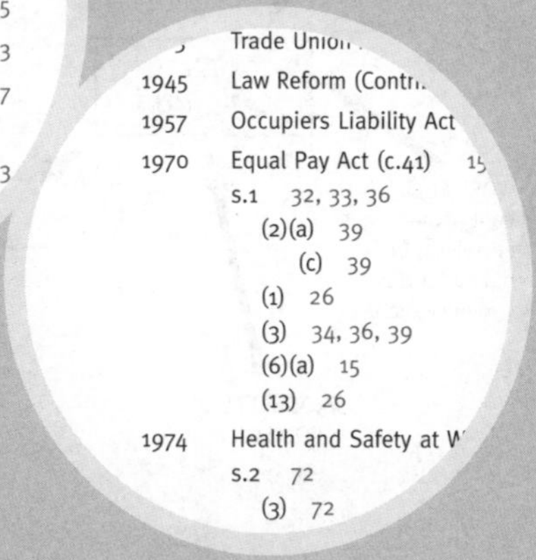

CHAPTER INTRODUCTIONS to outline the key concepts covered and condense complex and important information.

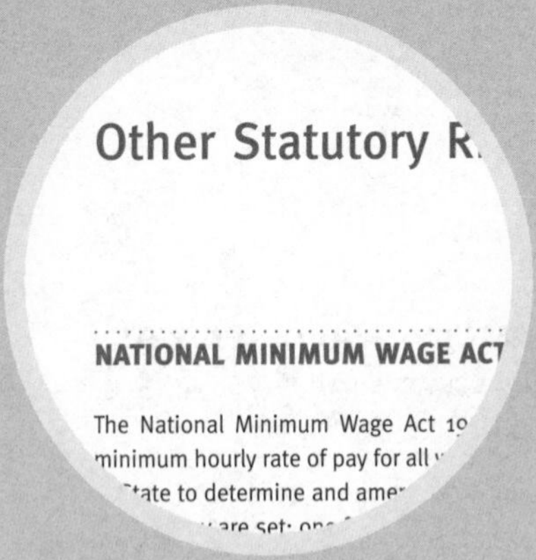

DIAGRAMS, FLOWCHARTS AND OTHER DIAGRAMMATIC REPRESENTATION to clarify and condense complex and important information and break up the text.

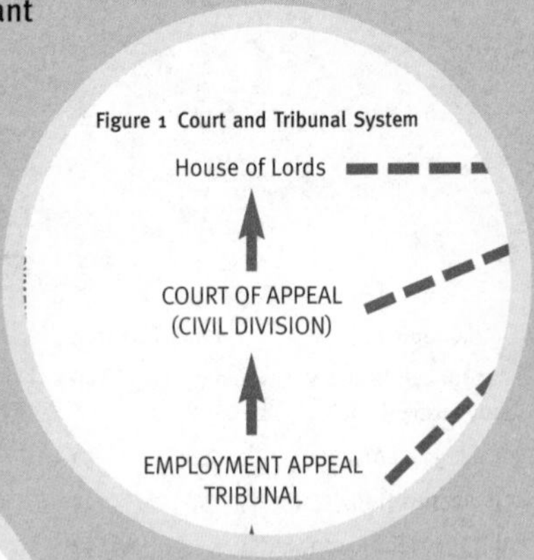

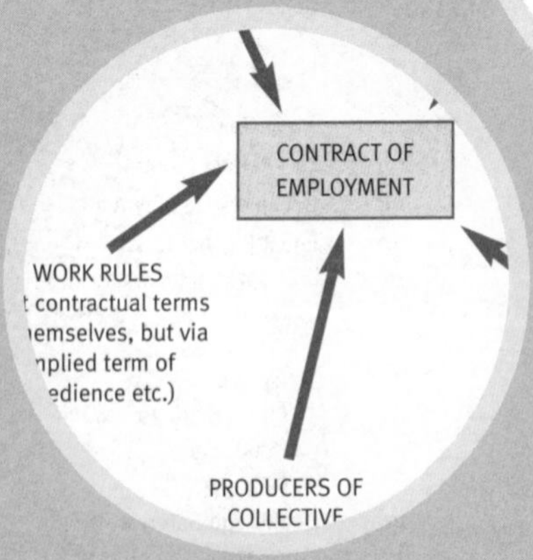

END OF CHAPTER REVISION CHECKLISTS outlining what you should now know and understand.

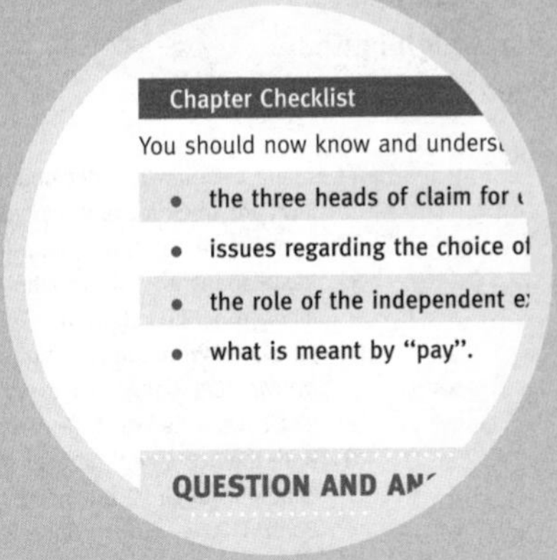
Chapter Checklist
You should now know and unders
the three heads of claim for
issues regarding the choice o
the role of the independent e
what is meant by "pay".
QUESTION AND AN

END OF CHAPTER QUESTION AND ANSWER SECTION with advice on relating knowledge to examination performance, how to approach the question, how to structure the answer, the pitfalls (and how to avoid them!) and how to get the best marks.

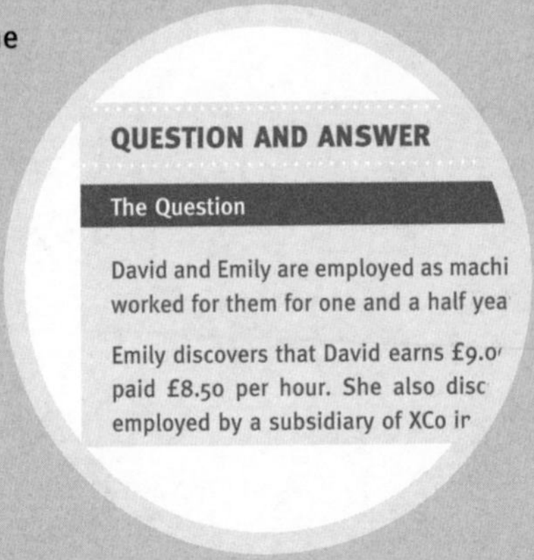
QUESTION AND ANSWER
The Question
David and Emily are employed as machi
worked for them for one and a half yea
Emily discovers that David earns £9.0
paid £8.50 per hour. She also disc
employed by a subsidiary of XCo ir

COLOUR CODING throughout to help distinguish cases and legislation from the narrative. At the first mention, cases are highlighted in colour and italicised and legislation is highlighted in colour and emboldened.

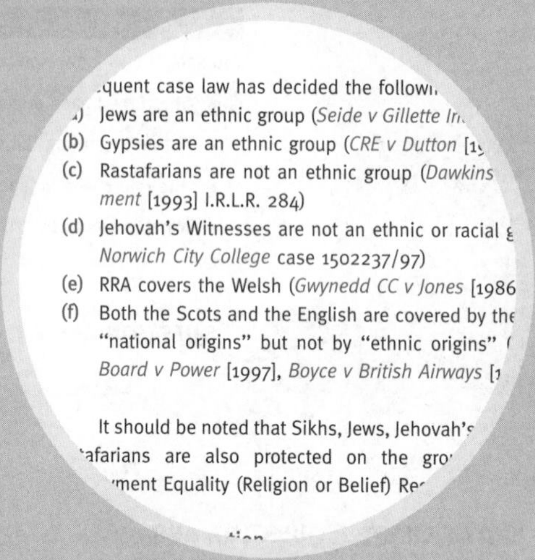
quent case law has decided the follow
Jews are an ethnic group (*Seide v Gillette*
(b) Gypsies are an ethnic group (*CRE v Dutton*
(c) Rastafarians are not an ethnic group (*Dawkins*
ment [1993] I.R.L.R. 284)
(d) Jehovah's Witnesses are not an ethnic or racial
Norwich City College case 1502237/97)
(e) RRA covers the Welsh (*Gwynedd CC v Jones* [1986
(f) Both the Scots and the English are covered by the
"national origins" but not by "ethnic origins"
Board v Power [1997], *Boyce v British Airways*
It should be noted that Sikhs, Jews, Jehovah's
afarians are also protected on the
ment Equality (Religion or Belief)

can readily understand and apply one another's substantive law and procedure.

CHARACTERISTICS SHARED BY COMMON LAW COUNTRIES

Adversarial procedure

The judge is an unbiased umpire. It is up to the parties to bring all the information the court needs to adjudicate. They research and construct the legal argument; they prepare and present factual and technical evidence and witness testimony, unaided by the court. The court does not investigate the case. For example, common law countries do not have anything like the French examining magistrate or Scottish procurator fiscal empowered to direct police investigations in serious criminal cases.

Importance of common law, judge-made law

The common law, made by judges, through the system of precedent, is just as important as statute law, codified law. Common law judges reason upwards from precedents not downwards from codes as judges do in civil law countries with codified law, such as France.

FURTHER READING

Darbyshire on the English Legal System, 10th edn, 2011, Sweet & Maxwell, and material cited and FURTHER READING listed therein.

Sources of Law

2

INTRODUCTION

This chapter is about sources of law:

- domestic legislation, including Acts and delegated legislation;
- EU law;
- the European Convention on Human Rights;
- statutory interpretation;
- case law;
- custom;
- books of authority; and
- international law.

DOMESTIC LEGISLATION

This means Acts of the UK Parliament and delegated legislation. When an Act is passed, it supersedes the common law. Since the mid-twentieth century, critics have argued that there is far too much legislation, especially delegated legislation, which is made by the executive, not the legislature. Happily, the number of new Acts and statutory instruments fell by eight per cent to 1,727, in 2011.

Acts of the UK Parliament

The best explanation of making statute law is on the UK Parliament website.

KEY POINT

Under the unwritten constitution, Parliament was given sovereign power by the **Act of Settlement 1700** but sovereignty is now qualified. Acts which run counter to EU law (formerly known as European Community law) may be suspended by the courts or declared invalid (*Factortame* (1991)). Otherwise, provided an Act has been passed by both Houses of Parliament, received Royal Assent and enrolled on to the parliamentary roll, it cannot be questioned by the courts. An exception occurs when the House of Lords (HL) refuses to pass a Bill. Under the **Parliament Act 1949**, it may be overridden and passed by the Commons only (e.g. the controversial **Hunting Act 2004**). Parliament cannot be bound by its predecessors or bind its successors.

Functions of Acts

Revision of substantive rules of law

Since 1965, the Law Commission has helped keep the law under review. Modernisation and simplification have been prompted by its reports or those of ad hoc Royal Commissions, or individuals, such as those of Leggatt on tribunals and Auld L.J. on criminal procedure.

Consolidation of enactments

Where law has evolved piecemeal, a single replacement Act can be passed without debate.

Codification

The enacting of rules of common law.

Collection of revenue

The annual Finance Act(s) implement the budget.

Social legislation

Enactments facilitating Government policy.

Forms of Acts

Distinguish between *public* Acts, of general effect, and *private* Acts, dealing with personal or local matters. Procedure differs. Distinguish between Government Bills (the majority), private Bills, hybrid Bills and private members' Bills, promoted by M.P.s or peers, selected by ballot. Matters of conscience (e.g. abortion) are often left by the Government to be dealt with in this way.

Validity of Acts

Parliamentary sovereignty precludes the courts' questioning Acts of Parliament where there is no conflict with EU law. The UK has no written constitution against which the courts could test their constitutionality, as does the Supreme Court in the US. An attempt was made to challenge the validity of the **Hunting Act 2004** but it was rejected: *R. (on the application of Jackson) v AG* [2005] UKHL 56. The **Human Rights Act 1998** permits the High Court and those above it (senior courts) to make a *declaration of incompatibility*, where they find an Act conflicts with the **European Convention on Human Rights 1950**. This triggers a fast-track remedial order procedure, under the **1998 Act** s.10. A Government minister may amend the offending Act, or subordinate legislation, subject to parliamentary approval. This preserves Parliamentary sovereignty.

Orders in Council

These are made by the executive government and have been held to be primary legislation, like an Act, not delegated legislation: *R (Bancoult) v SS for Foreign and Commonwealth Affairs (No 2)* [2008] UKHL 61 but they *are* reviewable by the courts, because this does not offend against parliamentary supremacy.

Welsh law

Under the **Government of Wales Act 1998**, the National Assembly for Wales, its legislature, was permitted to legislate in relation to matters within its devolved competence, such as agriculture, education, the environment, health, transport, housing, local government, sport and the Welsh language. The Assembly delegated many of its powers to its First Minister, who leads the Welsh Assembly Government. Under the **Government of Wales Act 2006**, the Assembly was given enhanced legislative power from 2011. The need to refer back to the UK Parliament was dispensed with. It should be remembered, however, that Welsh Acts, like Acts of the Scottish Parliament, are *delegated* legislation, reviewable by the UK Supreme Court.

Delegated legislation

Most delegated legislation takes the form of statutory instruments (SIs): rules and orders. Parliament has delegated power to other law-makers, mainly government ministers, in various Acts. Most statute law consists of SIs. There are sometimes over 3,000 per year, compared with under 100 Acts. Most EU law comes into the UK via SIs. Parliament also delegates law-making powers to public bodies and local government, enabling them to pass laws within their own field or locality, in the form of byelaws.

EUROPEAN UNION LEGISLATION

Sources

The European Communities Act 1972 (**ECA 1972**) provides that any UK enactment has effect subject to existing "enforceable Community rights" so, by implication, parliamentary sovereignty is limited to passing legislation which does not conflict with EU (Community) law. EU treaties are its primary source of law. They are binding on the EU institutions and Member States and, in certain circumstances, may create individual rights enforceable in national courts. The fundamental Treaty is the Treaty of Rome 1957. Article 288 of the **Treaty on the Functioning of the EU (TFEU)** (formerly art.249 of the **EC Treaty**), provides for secondary legislation:

Regulations have general, binding and direct applicability in all Member States.

Directives are binding, as to results to be achieved, upon each Member State to whom they are addressed, but leave form and methods to each Member State.

Decisions are binding on those to whom they are addressed.

APPLICABILITY AND ENFORCEMENT

Distinguish between *direct applicability* and *direct effect*. The former concept refers to the fact that all Treaty Articles and all Regulations immediately become part of the law of each Member State. The latter concept is the vehicle through which individuals may assert that, under EU law, they have rights which the Court of Justice of the European Union (CJEU) will protect, and upon which they can rely in national courts. The question as to whether a piece of legislation has *direct effect* is determined thus:

Treaty Articles

In the *Van Gend en Loos* case [1963] E.C.R. 1, The Court of Justice held the article in question created directly effective individual enforceable rights because:

- it was clear;
- it was unconditional; and
- its implementation required no further legislation in Member States.

Regulations

These have immediate applicability, becoming part of the law of each Member State. There is no need for further legislation to implement them. They are binding in their entirety and, like Treaty Articles, can be directly effective according to the above criteria.

Directives

The same *Van Gend* criteria have been applied to give *direct effect* to unimplemented Directives, where a person can show that they would have been granted a right under the Directive and they suffered a loss as a result of non-implementation. This only works where the applicant is acting against the State (and, as above, the provision is clear, precise, unconditional and leaves no room for discretion in implementation). The principle of direct effect cannot be implemented against a private party so there is no such thing as *horizontal* direct effect, confirmed in *Faccini Dori* [1995] All E.R. (EC) 1. Nevertheless, Directives have an *indirect effect*, in that national law may have to be reinterpreted to conform to them. The *Marleasing* case [1990] E.C.R. I-4135 held that national courts are bound by art.5 (now 10) EC to reconcile all national law, pre- or post-dating a Directive, in conformity with it. This has mitigated the results of the lack of horizontal direct effect. In *Francovich and Bonifaci v Italy* [1991] E.C.R. I-5357, the Court of Justice decided that an individual could sue the Member State where he had suffered loss as a result of non-implementation of a Directive.

Decisions

The Court of Justice has held that these may create individual rights which domestic courts must protect. They have direct applicability and may have direct effect.

Supremacy of EU law

KEY POINT

Under EU law, that law takes precedence over any earlier or later domestic law. In *Costa v ENEL* [1964] E.C.R. 585, the Court of Justice ruled that, in creating a Community with its own legal capacity, "the member states have limited their sovereign rights, albeit within limited fields, and have thus created a body of law which binds both their nationals and themselves". The **European Communities Act 1972 (ECA)** s.2 gives effect to EU law in the UK. Section 3(1) directs the UK courts to have regard to EU (Community) law. This includes the principle of supremacy. Where it appears to the UK courts that there is inadvertently conflicting UK legislation, they will endeavour to give effect to EU law.

The *Factortame* cases of 1990-91 (on Spanish fishing in UK waters) illustrate the power and significance of EU (Community) law. In 1990, on a reference for a preliminary ruling from the UK, the law lords, the Court of Justice opined that a UK court could suspend the application of any Act of Parliament on the grounds of its perceived incompatibility with EU law, and that EU law gave the national court the power to grant such interim relief, even though no such power existed in UK national law. Acting on this reference, the law lords confirmed that an interim injunction could be granted against the Crown, in such exceptional circumstances, to restrain it from enforcing an Act which apparently contravened EU law. The novelty here was the use of an injunction against the Crown since this was, otherwise, impossible.

Subsequently, in 1991, the Court of Justice indeed ruled that part of the Merchant Shipping Act 1988 ran counter to the EC Treaty, Treaty of Rome. The concept of an Act of Parliament's being declared not to be in conformity with EU law came as no news to lawyers in the UK, who were swift to point out that we gave up part of our sovereignty in the **ECA 1972**, but media reaction was scandalised.

THE EUROPEAN CONVENTION ON HUMAN RIGHTS 1950

KEY POINT

The **Convention** is a Treaty of the Council of Europe **NOT** an EU Treaty. It preceded the EU and has been ratified by a bigger group of states (47).

It was drafted by UK lawyers after World War II to protect basic freedoms and was made enforceable in the UK courts by the **Human Rights Act 1998** s.1. Its articles, as incorporated, are as follows:

1. Obligation to respect human rights.
2. Right to life.
3. Prohibition of torture.
4. Prohibition of slavery and forced labour.
5. Right to liberty and security.
6. Right to a fair trial.

7. No punishment without law.
8. Right to respect for private and family life.
9. Freedom of thought, conscience and religion.
10. Freedom of expression.
11. Freedom of assembly and association.
12. Right to marry.
13. Right to an effective remedy.
14. Prohibition of discrimination.
15. Restrictions on political activity of aliens.
16. Prohibition of abuse of rights.
17. Limitation on use of restrictions on rights.

- Some rights are absolute, such as art.3. Some admit exceptions, such as art.2. Most are subject to restrictions to ensure respect for other rights and freedoms.
- The **Human Rights Act 1998** s.2 provides that when a court or tribunal is determining a question in connection with a **Convention** right, it "must take into account" judgments, decisions or declarations of the European Court of Human Rights, or opinions or decisions of the Commission or the Committee of Ministers.
- Section 3 says "(s)o far as possible, primary legislation and subordinate legislation must be read and given effect in a way which is compatible with the Convention rights".
- Section 6 makes it unlawful for any public authority, including any court or tribunal, to act in a way incompatible with a **Convention** right.
- Any party to legal proceedings can rely on a **Convention** right. Whether the **Convention** confers horizontal rights (citizen against citizen) is, however, ambiguous, because while the interpretation obligation binds all citizens, ss.6 and 7 only allow challenges to actions of public authorities.

KEY POINT

Note the wording of s.3. Whereas EU law takes sovereign precedence over UK law, ***Convention** law does not*, because of this "let out" clause. There is no obligation on the courts, nor do they have the power, to *disapply* an Act of Parliament, but they are obliged to *reinterpret* legislation to comply, "where possible". If not, the High Court and above can make a declaration of incompatibility, under s.4(2).

These have been made a number of times. In *Bellinger v Bellinger* [2003] UKHL 23, the House of Lords declared that the non-recognition of gender reassignment, in English law, for the purposes of allowing a transsexual to marry, was incompatible with arts 8 and 12. The Government introduced the Gender Recognition Bill (now Act) .

STATUTORY INTERPRETATION

The need for interpretation

Statutory interpretation is necessary because Parliament can only be expected to provide a broad legal framework. It cannot spell out how an Act will apply in practice, in every set of circumstances. Bennion, in *Bennion on Statute Law* (1990) identified factors which can cause doubt as to meaning:

- Ellipsis: the deliberate omission of words that the draftsman thinks are implied. This causes no problem, provided all readers realise what is implied.
- Broad terms: where the draftsman uses generic terms, leaving the decision as to what falls into that category to the judge or statute user. For example, does the word "vehicle" cover a child's tricycle and a donkey cart?
- Politic uncertainty: where ambiguous words are used deliberately, where a provision is politically controversial or the Government lacks clear intent.
- Unforeseeable developments: where novel circumstances arise.
- Miscellaneous drafting errors: including accidental ambiguity and printing errors.

In *R v Chambers* [2008] EWCA Crim 2467, the Court of Appeal realised that for seven years no-one had noticed that the law on confiscating smuggled tobacco had changed. Over 1,000 confiscation orders were flawed. The CA said this was symptomatic of a wider problem. The law was inaccessible to everyone. Most of it was secondary legislation; the volume of legislation had increased and there was no comprehensive statute law database. (It is now on the legislation website but it is unclear whether it would satisfy this criticism.)

Traditional "rules" of interpretation

Judges do not employ *rules* of interpretation but common approaches have been identified and labelled as "rules". To some extent, judges select which "rule" to use in accordance with the result they seek to achieve in a case.

The literal rule

This approach involves giving words their ordinary, plain, natural meaning. In *Magnohard v Earl Cadogan and Cadogan Estates* [2012] EWCA Civ 594, the CA ruled that a "house" could not include a block of flats. In *Hosebay* [2012] UKSC 41, the Supreme Court held that a building used entirely for non-residential purposes could not be a "house". Sometimes judges feel constrained from reaching a just outcome by clear words. This occurred when Diane Blood was refused consent to use her dead husband's sperm because she lacked his written consent as required by the **Human Fertilisation and Embryology Act 1990**: *R. v Human Fertilisation and Embryology Authority Ex p. Blood* [1996] 3 W.L.R. 1176.

The golden rule

If words have more than one meaning, the least absurd is to be applied.

The mischief rule

This is commonly described as the last judicial approach, if the first two "rules" fail to assist. It is a much wider approach, determining the meaning of words by discovering the aim of the statute, the "mischief" at which the statute was directed. Under the contextual approach, below, the statute's aim is considered as part of the context of the words being interpreted.

The contextual approach

Sir Rupert Cross in *Statutory Interpretation* (1976 and later editions) described this judicial approach to statutory interpretation.

Considering the context

In giving words their ordinary or technical meaning or in delimiting broad terms, the judge must take them in their general context within the statute, and in the statute's external context. According to *Attorney General v Prince Ernest Augustus of Hanover* [1957] A.C. 436 ("the *Hanover* case") this includes the rest of the statute, the preamble, the existing state of the law and the factual context, i.e. the problem that the statute was intended to remedy. The statute must be read as a whole. Some judges refer to "a purposive approach", aiming to promote the general legislative purpose of a statute, to avoid, for example, ambiguities which would defeat its purpose, but this can only be done where judges can determine this from internal or external aids to interpretation (see below) and where such an approach is not defeated by presumptions of interpretation. An example of a contextual approach was *Laroche v Spirit of Adventure* [2009] EWCA Civ 12, the CA held that a hot air balloon was an "aircraft" according to the *Pocket Oxford Dictionary* but the plain, ordinary meaning was not necessarily determinative. On a purposive construction of the Carriage by Air Acts (Application of Provisions) Order 1967, it was reasonable to suppose that Parliament intended such balloons to be included as they were capable of being used for international transport.

Strict construction of criminal law

Penal statute law is construed strictly. The CA held there was no canon of statutory construction which empowered any court to write into a statute words which were not there, on the grounds that Parliament ought to have enacted a provision which it had not: *R. v Morgan R. v Bygrave* [2008] EWCA Crim 1323.

Modifying statutory language to avoid unreasonableness

The judge may read-in words which are necessarily implied and she has a limited power to add to, alter or ignore statutory words, to prevent a provision from being unintelligible, absurd, unreasonable, unworkable or totally irreconcilable with the rest of the statute, or to prevent a conflict with EU law or the **European Convention on Human Rights 1950**. According to case law, this approach should only rarely be necessary if, for example, there is a mistake in drafting, leading to an anomaly. There are a number of cases where the words "and" and "or" have been interchanged, to make sense of the statute. This approach was taken in *Inco Europe v First Choice Distribution* [2000] 1 W.L.R. 586 but the law lords warned that the purpose of the statute must be abundantly clear.

Rules of language

Ejusdem generis means a general word following a list of particular ones will normally be construed as restricted in scope to applying to things or persons of the same class (genus) as those listed, e.g. in *Powell v Kempton Park Racecourse Co* [1899] A.C. 143 it had to be decided whether "house, office, room or other place" included Tattersall's ring at the racecourse. It was held not to be included because "house, office, room" created a genus of indoor places so an outdoor racecourse could not fall within an "other place".

Noscitur a sociis means a word is to be construed as being similar to the rest of the objects in a list.

Expressio unius est exclusio alterius means that a specified member of a class impliedly excludes other members. For example, the inclusion of "coal mines" in this list: "lands, houses, tithes and coal mines" has been held to impliedly exclude other mines.

Internal aids to interpretation

Initial help may be found in the wording of the statute itself.

- Other enacting words. Another section may provide a clue to interpretation and there is often an interpretation section. For example, the Legal Aid, Sentencing and Punishment of Offenders Act 2012 defines such phrases as "legal aid".
- Long title. This sets out the aims of the Act. It can be as short as two lines, if the Act has one topic, or as long as a page, in a statute with diverse aims. Some Acts now contain an "overview", as does the Income Tax (Earnings and Pensions) Act 2003 s.1. (iii).
- Preamble. Some Acts, such as the Courts and Legal Services Act 1990, set out their purpose more clearly in a section. The preamble cannot prevail over clear enacting words.
- Short title, such as Finance Act 2012.
- Headings, side notes and punctuation. Although not voted on by Parliament, these are acceptable aids.

External aids

Judges may use some material external to the statute:

- Historical setting of the statute.
- Dictionaries and textbooks.
- Past practice.
- Related statutes.
- Previous statutes. Consolidating statutes are presumed not to alter the law but clear language may rebut this.
- Subordinate legislation.
- Government publications (with certain qualifications), e.g. Royal Commission or Law Commission reports and Government White Papers, in which the Government sets out the policy behind legislation. Statutes are now issued with explanatory notes. They appear alongside the Act on the Legislation website.
- Treaties and international conventions.
- Parliamentary materials. Until 1993, judges declined to refer to *Hansard*, the report of Parliamentary proceedings, but in *Pepper v Hart* [1993] A.C. 593 the House of Lords (HL), law lords, held that this rule

should be relaxed where legislation was ambiguous or obscure or the literal meaning led to an absurdity and, in identifying the true intention of the legislature, judges could be assisted by clear statements by the Bill's promoter. This principle has been applied more widely than intended. This was criticised by the HL in *R.v Secretary of State for the Environment, Transport and the Regions Ex p. Spath Holme Ltd.* [2001] 2 A.C. 349. Nevertheless, in *Wilson v First County Trust (No.2)* [2003] UKHL 40, the House extended the principle to decisions on compatibility with the **European Convention on Human Rights**.

Presumptions

General principles, such as the principles of natural justice (fair trial) and the principle that no one should be allowed to profit from their own crime, override even the clearest language. Presumptions, however, can be ousted by clear words. Parliament must spell out any intention to avoid the following presumptions:

- against changing the common law;
- against ousting the jurisdiction of the courts. The judges guard their own powers jealously and even some of the clearest "ouster" clauses have been held not to preclude judicial review;
- against interference with vested rights and freedoms (fundamental human rights) and that property cannot be taken away without compensation;
- against unduly penalising the citizen so criminal liability must be based on fault, unless clearly stated, and any penalty must be clear;
- against retrospective applicability;
- that statutes do not bind the Crown, so a common inclusion in an Act is a section specifically binding the Crown (e.g. the Royal family are not exempted from liability for traffic offences); and
- that Parliament does not intend to contravene the UK's international (Treaty) obligations, including the **European Convention on Human Rights**, the EU and EC treaties and so on.

The interpretation of EU law

The most important key to interpretation of EU law is the approach of the Court of Justice of the EU. The Court is more concerned with examining purpose and context than wording. The treaties are drafted in general terms, leaving it to the EU institutions, through secondary legislation, to fill in the details. The CJEU can review the legality of acts and omissions of EU institutions. It takes a dynamic approach in favour of the aims of the Union and the supremacy of EU law over national law, for example giving direct effect to

Directives. The Court employs a "rule of effectiveness" which means that preference should be given to the construction which gives a rule its fullest effect and it takes a contextual approach, referring to the general scheme of the Treaty or other Treaty provisions. Exceptions to EU rules and Treaty obligations are restrictively interpreted. For example, the principle of free movement of workers is limited by public policy, public security and public health, and these limitations are strictly construed.

The Court of Justice of the EU refers to "general principles of law", common to all Member States, derived from national law and the principles laid down by the European Court of Human Rights, which can be employed in the interpretation of Treaty provisions but which cannot override them. These principles include such things as proportionality, fair hearing, equality and legal certainty. The general principles of law are an important source of EU law and are used to interpret EU Treaties and when examining national law for conformity with the Treaties, as well as being almost a free standing source of law.

CASE LAW (PRECEDENT)

Significance

As we saw, much substantive law in the English legal system is the "common law", a creation of the judiciary through the application and development of case law and precedent. For example, the bulk of the law of tort and contract was developed as elements of common law, as well as important crimes such as murder and common assault. They are a creation of the judges and not of Parliament. This distinguishes the English legal system from the codified systems of Europe. Under the system of binding precedent or *stare decisis* (meaning "to stand by previous decisions") the lower courts are bound to apply the legal principles set down by the senior courts in earlier cases. This provides consistency and predictability and obviously depends on a system of law reporting. The part of a case which forms the binding precedent is:

- a statement of law (as opposed to fact);
- which forms part of the *ratio decidendi* (reason for the decision); and
- in a court whose decisions are binding.

The *ratio decidendi*

The *ratio decidendi* (plural, *rationes decidendi*) has been defined by Sir Rupert Cross, in *Precedent in English Law* (1961), thus:

> "any rule of law expressly or impliedly treated by the judge as a necessary step in reaching his conclusion, having regard to the line of reasoning adopted by him, or a necessary part of his direction to the jury".

The *ratio decidendi* (*ratio*) must be distinguished from an *obiter dictum* (plural, *dicta*) which is a statement of law not necessary for the decision in the case. A judge may decline or find it difficult to apply the *ratio decidendi* of a previous decision because:

- he does not agree with it and has managed to find discrepancies in the instant case which allow him to distinguish it from the precedent;
- no statements of principle appear in the precedent; or
- the *ratio* is difficult to extrapolate because different sets of reasoning have been used to found one decision, e.g. in HL or UK Supreme Court cases where there appear to be multiple *rationes decidendi* (e.g. *Hyam v DPP* [1975] A.C. 55; *Boys v Chaplin* [1969] 2 All E.R. 1085).

The function of the court hierarchy in the system of precedent

The Court of Justice of the European Union and the European Court of Human Rights

Under s.3 (1) of the **European Communities Act 1972** decisions of the CJEU (formally called the European Court of Justice, ECJ) are binding in matters of EU (Community) law on all UK courts. Under s.2 of the **Human Rights Act 1998** all UK courts must "take into account" the case law of the European Court of Human Rights when determining whether a **Convention** right has been breached. UK courts are not *bound* by the ECtHR. In 2009, in *Horncastle* [2009] UKSC 14, the UKSC declined to follow Strasbourg jurisprudence. In 2011, in *Al-Khawaja v UK* [2011] ECHR 2127, the ECtHR agreed with the UKSC that their interpretation was correct. Sir Nicholas Bratza, President of the ECtHR, said it was a good example of the judicial dialogue between the Court and national courts. See further M. Amos, at (2012) 61(3) I.C.L.Q. 557.

The UK Supreme Court (formerly appellate committee of the House of Lords)

Decisions of the UKSC/HL are binding on all the courts below it and, until 1966, were binding on later decisions of the House itself. In 1966, however, the Lords of Appeal (law lords) announced that they no longer intended to be bound by their previous decisions. This new, self-conferred power was intended to be used sparingly, to cater for revisions in law necessitated by changing social circumstances. It was such a change in societal attitudes which led to the first application of the new power, in *British Railways Board v Herrington* [1972] A.C. 877, strengthening tortious protection for child trespassers, when the harsh precedent of *Addie v Dumbreck* [1929] A.C. 358 was overturned. Since then, the House has used this power, or consciously declined to use it, on a number of occasions. In 2003, the House used its power to overrule the overly-wide *Caldwell* definition of recklessness, in *R. v G* [2003] UKHL 50. In 2006, it used this power in *Horton v Sadler* [2006] UKHL 27, to rule that a court has a wide power to disapply a statutory time-limit in a personal injury action. In *R (on the application of Purdy) v DPP* [2009] UKHL 45, they ruled that art.8(1) of the **E Conv HR** *was* engaged, when a terminally ill person sought assisted suicide, departing from their previous decision in *R on the application of Pretty v DPP* [2002] 1 All E.R. and instead following the ECtHR in *Pretty v UK* (2346/02) [2002] 2 F.C.R. 97.

The Court of Appeal (Civil Division)

The CA is bound by HL or UKSC decisions and its decisions are binding on all those courts below it.

Young v Bristol Aeroplane Company Ltd [1944] K.B. 718

The CA held itself to be bound by its own previous decisions, with three exceptions:

1. Decisions given *per incuriam* (through lack of care). This refers to decisions made in ignorance or forgetfulness of some statutory provision or some binding precedent, notably because it has not been brought to the court's attention.
2. Conflicting decisions of the CA. There is no consensus on which of two conflicting decisions, the earlier or the later, should be followed.
3. Decisions impliedly overruled by the HL, now UKSC.

Later case law added the following exception:

4. Decisions on interlocutory appeals, i.e. decisions taken by a Court of Appeal of only two judges.

Smith, Bailey & Gunn on the Modern English Legal System (Sweet & Maxwell, latest edition) lists, in addition, the following possible exceptions to *Young v Bristol Aeroplane*:

5. Inconsistency with an earlier HL decision: the HL (or UKSC) decision is binding.
6. Inconsistency with a Privy Council decision. This, however, is a dubious creation of Lord Denning M.R.
7. Inconsistency with international law. International law must be followed.
8. Where the CA is the court of last resort, with no appeal available to the HL/UKSC.
9. The HL in *Davis v Johnson* [1979] A.C. 264 reaffirmed the rule that, other than in these cases, the CA is bound by its own previous decisions. (See also *Rickards v Rickards* [1990] Fam. 194).

The Court of Appeal (Criminal Division)

This division is bound by the UKSC (formerly HL), by itself and by its historic predecessors, unless it is a CA decision falling into one of the exceptions in *Young v Bristol Aeroplane*. Further, the CA said in *R. v Spencer* [1987] A.C. 128 that, where they were dealing with the liberty of the subject, they would depart from authority in the interests of justice to the appellant. Sometimes, the CA regrets being bound by the House of Lords/UKSC where the law clearly needs reforming and Parliament has not spared the time to do so: *A v Hoare* [2006] EWCA Civ 395. A "full court" of five Lord Justices has the power to overrule a previous decision of a court of three. Full courts have been used regularly in recent years. It is uncertain whether the two divisions of the CA bind each other but in some instances they have manifested an intention not to be so bound, for example, in their conflicting approach towards the constitutionality of jury vetting in *R. v Sheffield Crown Court Ex p. Brownlow* [1980] Q.B. 530 and *R. v Mason* [1980] 3 W.L.R. 617.

The High Court

It is bound by the CA and HL/UKSC but is not bound by other HC decisions, with the exception below.

Divisional Courts of the High Court

Divisional Courts of the HC are, when exercising their *appellate* function, binding on their successors and amenable to the principles in *Young v Bristol Aeroplane* but not when exercising their judicial review function: *R. v Greater Manchester Coroner Ex p. Tal* [1984] Q.B. 67.

The Crown Court, magistrates' courts and county courts

These decisions are seldom reported and are not binding on any court.

Tribunals

Upper Tribunal and appellate decisions are binding on the chambers below them.

Persuasive precedents

Precedents which are not binding may be taken as persuasive and, indeed, have played a significant part in assisting judicial creativity where there are gaps in the law, a classic example being the development of liability for negligent misstatements resulting in pure economic loss, from an *obiter* statement of the HL. The following precedents are persuasive:

1. *Obiter dicta* of the HL/UKSC.
2. Decisions of the Judicial Committee of the Privy Council (JCPC). In a unique decision, *R. v James, R. v Karimi* [2005] EWCA Crim 14, the Court of Appeal decided to follow a JCPC decision instead of an earlier, binding, HL decision. The JCPC had decided in *R. v Holley* [2005] UKPC 23, an appeal from Jersey, that the HL precedent on provocation in murder, *R. v Smith (Morgan)* [2001] 1 A.C. 146 had been wrongly decided. The CA chose to follow the persuasive JCPC decision, predicting that, if it did not, the HL (comprised of the same judges as the JCPC) would overrule it.
3. Decisions from other common law jurisdictions.
4. Textbooks.
5. Judgments of parallel courts, where these are not binding, for example, the High Court.

Judges as law makers

There has been a perpetual debate about whether judges can and should make the law, in statutory interpretation, as well as in developing precedent. This is really a topic for a constitutional law book but for a recent examination see P. Sales, "Judges and legislature: values into law" (2012) 71 (2) C.L.J. 287, *Westlaw*.

PREROGATIVE POWER

This type of power is a residue of the power formally exercised by the monarch. It is normally exercised by ministers. It is not trivial or obscure. It includes such important matters as the conduct of foreign relations and the power to wage war and peace. Because these powers are historic and not prescribed in writing, their vagueness is perceived by critics as undesirable, as it is solely defined by the courts and then only when its use is challenged. When a statute is passed on the same topic as a prerogative power, the courts assume that the Act has superseded the prerogative power.

CUSTOM

The common law of England was derived from the customary laws of Anglo-Saxon kingdoms. Custom rarely plays a part in modern England and Wales, except where the court is prepared to accept evidence of established custom, as a defence. It sometimes helps develop elements of international commercial law, however, such as banking.

BOOKS OF AUTHORITY

Modern, authoritative, well-established textbooks, such as Smith & Hogan's *Criminal Law*, and practitioner texts such as *Archbold* on criminal law and procedure, are often relied on as dependable statements of the law because of the expertise of those who wrote them. Similarly, ancient books of authority are occasionally cited.

INTERNATIONAL LAW

Private international law covers private relations, such as family affairs. Public international law governs relations between states. It becomes binding in English law when the UK government signs and then ratifies the treaty that has created it. The courts take a purposive approach to construction. International law, where the UK is a contracting party, overrides domestic common law.

Revision Checklist

You should now know and understand:

- the sources of domestic law: Acts of the UK Parliament, Welsh law, Orders in Council, delegated legislation, especially bylaws and statutory instruments, case law, prerogative power, custom and books of authority;
- the **European Convention on Human Rights** and how it was made applicable in the UK by the **Human Rights Act 1998**;
- EU law and the mechanism by which it was and is incorporated into UK law, as prescribed in the **European Communities Act 1972**;
- the concept of sovereignty of the UK Parliament and how this is subordinate to the sovereignty of EU law;
- the hierarchy of precedent and the way precedent works;
- the approach judges take in interpreting statute law, using rules and presumptions, internal and external aids and context; and
- the different statutory powers and interpretive approaches of the courts in EU law and Convention law, remembering that the latter preserves UK Parliamentary sovereignty and remembering that the **European Convention on Human Rights** is *not* a Treaty of the EU.

FURTHER READING/UPDATING

Darbyshire on the ELS, 2011, material cited and FURTHER READING listed therein and web updates on the Sweet & Maxwell website.

C. Manchester and D. Salter, *Exploring the Law* (latest edition)

Statute Law Review

Times law reports

Websites

Council of Europe

Europa

Francis Bennion

Welsh Assembly Government

Legislation website for statute law. Amended, annotated statute law is on *Lexis* and *Westlaw*.

UK Parliament: excellent, informative website and one cannot better its factual information on the legislative process, which is why the information is not repeated here.

QUESTION AND ANSWER

Question

'While the common law is a very important source of law, the many other sources of English law are growing in importance'.

Advice and the Answer

Advice

This question is a gift. It is a very straightforward test of knowledge of the sources of law but it does require some thought to evaluate the IMPORTANCE of the common law now, relative to all the other sources.

Answer guide

1. Explain what common law is. Historically, it meant the law promulgated by the royal courts in Westminster and commonly applied throughout the kingdom of England, from around the Norman Conquest, distinct from canon law (church law) and the local systems of customary law from the tiny historic kingdoms from which England was formed. Nowadays, common law means law developed and applied by judges on a case by case basis, in the system of precedent.
2. Briefly explain how judges develop common law principles through precedent.
3. Give examples of judge-made common law, commenting on their *importance*, because the question requires an evaluation of importance. Obvious examples are the basic rules of contract, the whole of the law of tort and common law crimes, such as murder. You can draw on your knowledge of important modern cases. For example, the law lords, then the UK Supreme Court have been very outspoken about torture and reminding us of the common law hostility to torture in their judgments from 2005.
4. Mention that judge-made common law is important as a source of law not just in England and Wales but throughout the common law world because English common law has formed the base of substantive law and procedure not just in England but in all her common law daughter jurisdictions. Also, briefly explain how common law principles are developed on a worldwide basis.

5. Then turn to the other sources of law. The more the common law is replaced by codified law—statutes, statutory instruments, international treaties and European Community law, the more it retreats into the background and diminishes in importance.
6. You can visit the Legislation website and explain how many Acts and statutory instruments are made each year and see how many more there are now than decades earlier.
7. Having said that, judge-made law is still much more important in common law countries than in European civil law jurisdictions, because the base of their law comprises principles embodied in codes, whereas our principles are articulated and developed by judges in the system of binding precedent.
8. Remember to explain and evaluate the importance of all the sources of law explained in this chapter.
9. EU law is very important indeed, since 1972/3, because it is sovereign over all domestic law and the ambit of the European Community then the EU has expanded since then, covering more areas of our lives. Examine the wording of the **1972 Act** and the relevant judgments of the Court of Justice of the EU, formerly ECJ, to show that the concept of sovereignty of EU law derives from both domestic law and EU law.
10. The **European Convention on Human Rights** has been recognised since the 1950s, when the UK ratified the **Convention** but grown in importance very significantly since our courts were empowered to enforce it from 2000, by dint of the **1998 Act**. Give practical examples of its influence on our domestic law but it is also well worth pointing out that the content of the articles is clearly derived from common law rules (e.g. see chapter on criminal procedure). UK lawyers drafted the **Convention** and took the principles from common law. The **Convention** is now applied in 47 contracting states so it has had an extremely important indirect influence, which is hardly ever acknowledged.
11. Remember to explain the importance of statutory interpretation and, briefly, the principles and presumptions.
12. Do not forget to assess the importance of international law. London is a major international centre. With globalisation, international law takes on a greater importance.
13. Explain the modern significance of prerogative power. Historically, it was of major importance because it was power exercised by the monarch. Although Acts of Parliament supersede the prerogative, prerogative power is not obscure, or merely

historic. It governs the whole of foreign relations, such as declarations of war and peace.

14. Explain: while custom was very important in the development of the common law, it is far less important now, though it does help develop international law.
15. Reach a brief conclusion based on what you have just argued.

THE COURT STRUCTURE

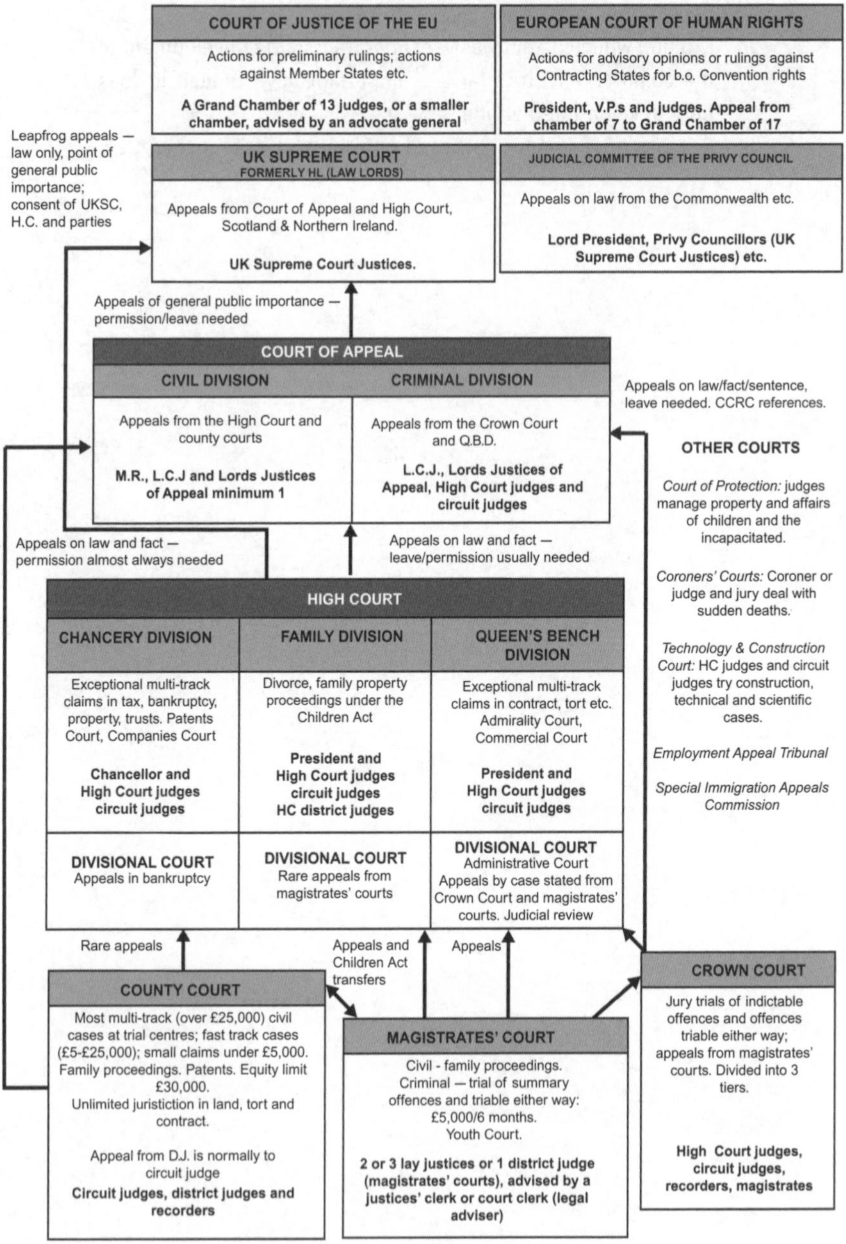

COURT OF JUSTICE OF THE EU
Actions for preliminary rulings; actions against Member States etc.
A Grand Chamber of 13 judges, or a smaller chamber, advised by an advocate general
EUROPEAN COURT OF HUMAN RIGHTS
Actions for advisory opinions or rulings against Contracting States for b.o. Convention rights
President, V.P.s and judges. Appeal from chamber of 7 to Grand Chamber of 17
Leapfrog appeals — law only, point of general public importance; consent of UKSC, H.C. and parties
UK SUPREME COURT
FORMERLY HL (LAW LORDS)
Appeals from Court of Appeal and High Court, Scotland & Northern Ireland.
UK Supreme Court Justices.
JUDICIAL COMMITTEE OF THE PRIVY COUNCIL
Appeals on law from the Commonwealth etc.
Lord President, Privy Councillors (UK Supreme Court Justices) etc.
Appeals of general public importance — permission/leave needed
COURT OF APPEAL
CIVIL DIVISION
Appeals from the High Court and county courts
M.R., L.C.J and Lords Justices of Appeal minimum 1
CRIMINAL DIVISION
Appeals from the Crown Court and Q.B.D.
L.C.J., Lords Justices of Appeal, High Court judges and circuit judges
Appeals on law/fact/sentence, leave needed. CCRC references.
OTHER COURTS
Court of Protection: judges manage property and affairs of children and the incapacitated.
Coroners' Courts: Coroner or judge and jury deal with sudden deaths.
Technology & Construction Court: HC judges and circuit judges try construction, technical and scientific cases.
Employment Appeal Tribunal
Special Immigration Appeals Commission
Appeals on law and fact — permission almost always needed
Appeals on law and fact — leave/permission usually needed
HIGH COURT
CHANCERY DIVISION
Exceptional multi-track claims in tax, bankruptcy, property, trusts. Patents Court, Companies Court
Chancellor and High Court judges circuit judges
DIVISIONAL COURT
Appeals in bankruptcy
FAMILY DIVISION
Divorce, family property proceedings under the Children Act
President and High Court judges circuit judges HC district judges
DIVISIONAL COURT
Rare appeals from magistrates' courts
QUEEN'S BENCH DIVISION
Exceptional multi-track claims in contract, tort etc. Admirality Court, Commercial Court
President and High Court judges circuit judges
DIVISIONAL COURT
Administrative Court
Appeals by case stated from Crown Court and magistrates' courts. Judicial review
Rare appeals
Appeals and Children Act transfers
Appeals
COUNTY COURT
Most multi-track (over £25,000) civil cases at trial centres; fast track cases (£5-£25,000); small claims under £5,000. Family proceedings. Patents. Equity limit £30,000.
Unlimited juristiction in land, tort and contract.
Appeal from D.J. is normally to circuit judge
Circuit judges, district judges and recorders
MAGISTRATES' COURT
Civil - family proceedings.
Criminal — trial of summary offences and triable either way: £5,000/6 months.
Youth Court.
2 or 3 lay justices or 1 district judge (magistrates' courts), advised by a justices' clerk or court clerk (legal adviser)
CROWN COURT
Jury trials of indictable offences and offences triable either way; appeals from magistrates' courts. Divided into 3 tiers.
High Court judges, circuit judges, recorders, magistrates

The Court Structure

3

INTRODUCTION

KEY BACKGROUND POINTS

- It is not a coherent, logically developed "system". It grew piecemeal because the history of the ELS is such a long one.
- The distribution of work between courts and tribunals is somewhat arbitrary but was not questioned until the Leggatt Report, 2001.
- We seldom question whether we need two criminal and two civil courts of first instance (trial courts). Auld L.J. did so in the Criminal Courts Review, 2001.
- Most civil cases are settled out of court, by negotiation, or dealt with by ADR, or arbitration, or allocated by statute to a tribunal.
- Most criminal offences committed by young people (and some by adults) result in a caution or a fixed penalty.
- Most civil cases were shifted down into county courts, following **The Courts and Legal Services Act 1990**, reserving the High Court for complex, important or specialist cases.
- Criminal cases have shifted down into the magistrates' courts over the last three centuries.
- **The Crime and Courts Bill 2012**, if enacted and implemented, will create a single county court and a single family court for England and Wales. A single family court has been discussed since the 1960s and promised by many governments.
- Open justice: sound and video recordings and photography were banned by statute. Free, live coverage of the UKSC has been provided since its creation. **The above Bill** will, if enacted, enable rules to be made permitting the broadcasting of court proceedings.

CRIMINAL COURTS

Magistrates' courts

These are the most important criminal courts because they dispose of around 95 per cent of criminal business. In Outer London and the provinces, most cases are heard by unrobed lay justices (lay magistrates), sitting in twos or threes, advised by a justices' clerk or court clerk, known as a legal adviser. In Inner London, most cases are heard by a professional district judge (magistrates' courts) (DJMC).

Of these criminal cases, many are *summary* traffic offences, most of which are decided in the absence of the defendant, who may plead guilty by post. The Coalition Government proposes permitting single magistrates to deal with these. Another quarter are *triable either way* offences, cases of median seriousness, where the defendant has the option of a Crown Court appearance instead. The rest are other summary offences. Magistrates hear almost all cases against young people aged 10–17, in private, in the youth court. Some are heard in the Crown Court, as explained in the criminal procedure chapter. There are over 29,000 unpaid lay magistrates, who sit part-time in around 246 courts in England and Wales, and around 137 professional magistrates, DJMCs.

Criticisms

- It is an accident of history that most cases are dealt with in Inner London by a DJMC, often advised by a professionally qualified clerk, yet in Outer London and the provinces, the same work is mainly done by lay justices whose legal advisers are not always barristers or solicitors.
- Parliament and the senior judiciary often make the mistake of developing the law as if most criminal cases were still heard by judge and jury in the Crown Court.
- From 2009, virtual courts were piloted, trying the defendant on a video link from the police station and, if he pleads guilty, sentencing him where possible. The 2010 decision to extend them was criticised, since they cost more. There are (October 2012) 48 "flexible (experimental) pilots".
- Over 100 local courts were closed by the Coalition Government in 2010–12, supposedly to save money. This destroys localism and makes courts less accessible. Local magistrates have been providing justice for local people for 600 years. The Magistrates' Association opposed the cuts (see website).
- Governments are always trying to shift more cases down into these

courts from the much more expensive Crown Court, as explained in Chapter 6 on criminal procedure.

- The Coalition's 2012 white paper says "Up to 100 magistrates' courts are sitting on Saturdays and Bank Holidays, reducing delays and delivering swift, sure, flexible justice" but (I would add) weekend and evening courts have been experimented with since the 1970s and they are a burden on court users—magistrates, legal advisers, staff, police, lawyers and probation officers.

Community Justice Centres

The first was opened in 2004, in Liverpool, copying an American project. There are ten more. Local people help select the judge. The CJC has the jurisdiction of a magistrates' court and is meant to involve the community in tackling crime and anti-social behaviour. One theme is restorative justice.

Drugs Courts and Domestic Violence Courts

Drugs courts commenced with two experimental courts and have been replicated. Offenders convicted of low level crime can be sent for sentencing. By 2011 there were 140 specialist domestic violence courts, with support services for victims.

The Crown Court

This is the criminal court of first instance, dealing with the most serious (*indictable*) offences, as well as some *either way* offences. It hears appeals from magistrates' courts. It replaced assizes and quarter sessions, following the **Courts Act 1971**. There is one Crown Court, divided between about 89 centres in six circuits, in three tiers:

First tier

High Court (HC) judges deal with the most serious offences.

Second tier

HC judges may sit.

Third tier

HC judges do not normally visit.

Most work is handled by circuit judges. Recorders (part-timers) may sit in all tiers. If there is a trial, guilt is determined by a jury of 12. Appeals are heard by a judge and two lay magistrates.

KEY POINT

There are three main categories of criminal case

- Summary (least serious) heard in the magistrates' court.
- Triable either way (either way) heard in the magistrates' court or Crown Court.
- Indictable (most serious) heard in the Crown Court.

The Queen's Bench Division of the High Court (QBD)

Its Divisional Court, with two or three judges, hears *appeals by way of case stated* from the magistrates' court and the Crown Court (except in relation to CC trials) and, in the Administrative Court, it exercises *supervisory jurisdiction* over certain matters in the Crown Court and magistrates' courts, i.e. judicially reviewing the legality of their proceedings and orders.

The Court of Appeal (Criminal Division)

This is presided over by the Lord Chief Justice (L.C.J.) and its Vice-President. It normally comprises one of the 37 Lords Justices, plus two HC judges. Important appeals are heard by five judges. Certain circuit judges are authorised ("ticketed") to sit. It hears appeals on fact, law and sentence. Appeals against sentence may be heard by two judges. It normally sits in the Royal Courts of Justice in the Strand, London but has sat in Cardiff, Liverpool and elsewhere.

The UK Supreme Court (UKSC), formerly House of Lords Appellate Committee

It was created in October 2009 by the **Constitutional Reform Act 2005**, in Parliament Square, in order to enhance the constitutional separation of powers, replacing the *law lords* who were, historically, a committee of the House of Lords. It hears *points of law of general public importance*, including civil appeals from Scotland and civil and criminal appeals from Northern Ireland. There are always two Justices from Scotland and one from NI. The minimum number determining an appeal is three but normally five, or up to nine for important cases. As well as the maximum of 12 fulltime Justices, acting judges may be drawn from senior judges or retired Justices. The Court may be assisted by specially qualified advisers.

Background

In 2003, the Department for Constitutional Affairs proposed the replacement of the HL Appellate Committee with a Supreme Court and, after much debate, this was achieved in the **2005 Act**. The Government was keen to remove breaches of the separation of powers (executive/legislature/judiciary). It considered that judicial independence, required by art.6 of the **European Convention on Human Rights 1950**, necessitated removing the historic link between the law lords (judiciary) and Parliament (legislature). This had been advocated by two law lords, Lords Bingham and Steyn. There was no intention to create a court like the US Supreme Court, with a power to overturn legislation. The court does the same work as the law lords. Most of the first Justices were law lords. Additionally, it was given jurisdiction over devolution cases formerly exercised by the JCPC. Opponents regretted the loss of the law lords' right to speak in Parliament, on law reform.

The Judicial Committee of the Privy Council (JCPC)

It moved to the UKSC building in 2009. It hears appeals from some Commonwealth countries and from some professional bodies. It comprises the Lord President of the Council, UKSC Justices and former Privy Councillors who have held high judicial office in the UK or Commonwealth, or current Commonwealth judges. Normally, a board of five sits.

Criticism

Commentators suggested the JCPC's jurisdiction in death penalty appeals from the Caribbean was inappropriate for modern, European judges and their views often conflicted with those of the inhabitants of islands from which appeals are sent. For instance, in 2006, it abolished the mandatory death penalty in the Bahamas: *Bowe v The Queen* [2006] UKPC 10. Human rights QC, Keir Starmer, said this was the culmination of a ten-year litigation strategy to abolish the death penalty in the Caribbean. For this reason, some Caribbean countries have created their own Court of Justice.

The Court of Justice of the European Union (CJEU), formerly European Court of Justice (ECJ)

It sits in Luxembourg and consists of 27 judges, one from each EU state. The most important cases are heard by a Grand Chamber of 13. One peculiar feature, unknown to English law, is the function of the Advocates General. One Advocate General sits with the bench in each hearing and may question the parties, delivering an opinion some weeks later. This sets out facts, law and a suggested judgment. The court contains a General Court (formerly Court of First Instance) which has 27 judges. It hears actions against EU institutions, cases on state aid, dumping, actions for damages and so on. Its jurisdiction is on the Europa website.

The Court of Justice hears:

- applications from Member States' courts for preliminary rulings on EU law;
- actions against Member States for failure to fulfil obligations;
- actions for annulment of regulations, directives or decisions;
- review actions for EU institutions' failure to act; and
- appeals on points of law from the General Court and certain reviews.

The European Court of Human Rights (ECtHR)

KEY POINT

This court is NOT an institution of the EU and should not be confused with the Court of Justice of the EU, above.

It sits in Strasbourg and enforces states' obligations under the **European Convention on Human Rights 1950** for those 47 *contracting states* which have ratified this treaty, including the UK. The UK has been taken before the court on many occasions, necessitating amendments in domestic law. It has 47 judges, one from each state. They sit in chambers of seven or, for important cases and appeals from a chamber decision, a Grand Chamber of 17.

Criticism

Led by the UK, a group of contracting states were concerned that the Court was interfering far too much in domestic law and policy, and that its judges were not sufficiently qualified, bearing no comparison with the highly qualified and internationally respected judges of the UKSC and other top courts. As a result of a 2012 conference, the 47 states agreed to a package of reforms called the "Brighton declaration", including amending the **Convention** to include the principles of subsidiarity and the margin of appreciation. This means that contracting states have to be left to manage their own affairs as much as possible. The Court will tighten the admissibility criteria, focusing on serious cases, reduce the claim time limit to four months, and improve the selection of judges. The then Minister of Justice, Ken Clarke, said this would help to stop the "scandalous delays" in handling cases. Some members of the Conservative party criticise the reach of the **Convention**. In 2011, the Coalition government established a Commission on a Bill of Rights, to consider creating a UK Bill of Rights. This is enormously controversial and has been heavily discussed in the media and law journals in 2011–12.

CIVIL COURTS

KEY POINT

Civil, non-family cases, if defended, are allocated to one of three tracks

- small claims, under £5,000, heard by district judges at the county court
- fast track, under £25,000, heard by DJs or circuit judges in the county court
- multi-track, heard by DJs or CJs or HC judges, in county court trial centres, or district registries of the HC, or in the HC in London.

In 2012, the Coalition Government is proposing raising the small claims and fast track limits, as part of the Jackson reforms, discussed in Chapter 4.

Civil courts include the UKSC, the JCPC, the CJEU and the ECtHR, as described above.

Magistrates' courts

They have a significant civil case load, predominantly in the Family Proceedings Court. Lay justices who hear family cases are selected from specially trained panels. DJMCs may sit alone. All are empowered to make and enforce most orders ancillary to a divorce, such as money orders. Under the Children Act 1989, they have the same powers over children as the HC and county courts, so they can make residence and contact orders, and so on.

County courts

These are the most important courts for most people involved in a civil case as they handle most civil business. They were created in 1846, as a cheaper, simpler, local alternative to the HC. There are 218 after closures. Their jurisdiction is set out in the **Courts and Legal Services Act 1990** and delegated legislation. It consists of cases on contract, tort, property, divorce and other family matters, bankruptcy, admiralty, equity, probate, race relations, etc. Many are debt claims. Solicitors have rights of audience in all cases. Most cases are managed or heard by county court DJs, others by circuit judges or recorders. All types of judge sit alone, except in rare trials where liability is determined by a jury. Some big courts have been renamed *civil justice centres* because they also offer ADR (alternative dispute resolution).

The High Court

It sits in the Royal Courts of Justice (Strand) (RCJ) and at provincial courts.

The Queen's Bench Division

This is the largest, generalist division, consisting of the President of the QBD and about 71 HC judges. It deals with common law (tort and contract) and actions for recovery of land and property. It contains two specialist courts, Admiralty and Commercial, and it administers the Technology and Construction Court. It sits in London and some district registries at county courts. The Divisional Court of the QBD hears some appeals from the magistrates' courts and the Crown Court and exercises the supervisory jurisdiction, judicially reviewing the legality of the actions of the lower courts and, in the Administrative Court, public bodies such as central and local government. Outside the Divisional Court, all HC judges sit alone, except in rare tort cases, where they may sit with a jury.

The Chancery Division

This consists of the Chancellor of the HC and 19 HC judges. It hears claims relating to property, trusts, wills, partnerships, revenue, contentious probate, company and personal insolvency, intellectual property and copyright. It includes two specialist courts, Patent and Companies. It sits in London and in eight provincial centres. Its Divisional Court hears bankruptcy and insolvency appeals. Some appeals have shifted to the Finance and Tax Chamber of the Upper Tribunal from 2009, which is staffed by Chancery Division judges.

The Family Division

This consists of the President of the Family Division and 19 HC judges who hear divorce cases and ancillary matters and **Children Act** cases in London and district registries of county courts. There are about 20 HC *district* judges at the Principal Registry of the FD in Holborn, London, not to be confused with county court DJs.

Other Elements of the High Court

Some tribunals are also superior courts of record, part of the HC, such as the Employment Appeal Tribunal.

The Court of Appeal (Civil Division)

It hears appeals on fact and law from the HC and county courts. It is headed by the Master of the Rolls, who is Head of Civil Justice. Lords Justices of Appeal may sit alone, or in pairs or threes, or fives, dependent on the seriousness of the appeal. It sits in the RCJ and occasionally in Cardiff.

COURT MANAGEMENT

The Ministry of Justice runs the courts. The Justice Secretary, a Cabinet minister, is also the Lord Chancellor (in 2012, an M.P., though the L.C. may be from the House of Lords). He is assisted by junior ministers. They develop policy and promote and make relevant legislation, and the Justice Secretary is answerable to Parliament. Her Majesty's Courts and Tribunals Service, an independent government agency, administers the courts on a day-to-day basis. Judges are concerned that the courts budget is continually reduced, in real terms, and from the 1990s governments developed policy that the civil courts should pay for themselves. Judges consider that the courts should be provided as a public (social) service, as they are in other countries.

OPEN COURTS

Courts should be open to the public, under art.6 of the **European Convention on Human Rights**, with certain exceptions, such as national security, children and family privacy. Until 2009, access to family courts was patchy and confusing. Some family proceedings are now open, if permitted by the judge, and may be reported, with restrictions. The UKSC provides a live broadcast of proceedings, under the **Constitutional Reform Act 2005**. It is illegal to photograph or film proceedings but see the key background point above.

Revision Checklist

With the help of the court structure diagram, you should now understand:

- **the court structure and how courts relate to the European Court of Human Rights, the Court of Justice of the EU and the UKSC;**
- **the distribution of civil and criminal work, in outline;**
- **which judges sit in which courts; and**
- **why the UKSC was created.**

FURTHER READING/UPDATING

Darbyshire on the ELS, 2011, Chapters 6 and 7 and web updates
Civil Justice Review 1988
Court of Justice of the EU, Europa website
Court structure diagram
Criminal Courts Review 2001
ECtHR website
HM Courts and Tribunals Service website and some courts have their own websites, such as the Old Bailey, the UKSC and the JCPC

Magistrates' Association website
Ministry of Justice website

QUESTION AND ANSWER

The Question

'The English court structure is not a faultlessly coherent, logical system'. Discuss.

Advice and the Answer

Advice

1. Read the general guidance at the back of this book.
2. Study the court structure diagram and the chapters on civil and criminal procedure, as they are also relevant.
3. Read more widely.
4. There are arguments both ways, otherwise this point would not have been raised for discussion.

Answer guide

1. Explain that the court structure is very old and has been continually developing since before 1066 so it cannot be expected to be as faultlessly coherent as a newly-designed court structure.
2. Examine the ways in which it *is* coherent. It is fairly clear which cases are heard in which courts. It is fairly logical, with two civil courts of first instance and two criminal courts of first instance. Generally, business is distributed between them sensibly thanks to successive reforms, with the lower, cheaper courts handling most business, in fairly swift procedures, heard by unpaid lay magistrates and the lowest ranking judges, DJs. The HC is reserved for unusually complex or expensive civil cases and the Crown Court handles serious crime. Appeals are heard at an appropriate level (especially since the reform of civil appeals in 1999, as explained in the civil procedure chapter), with the top court being reserved for cases of points of law of general public importance. There are specialist courts with knowledgeable judges, such as the Commercial Court and the Technology and Construction Court.

3. Progressive piecemeal reforms, like the redistribution of civil and criminal cases and the creation of the UKSC (explain why and how), have made the system more logical and coherent.
4. Nevertheless, there are deficiencies in coherence and logic.

    a. Family cases, especially children cases, may start in one of three courts and often, parents whose relationship is breaking up may need to appear in two or three types of court, which is very confusing, stressful and time consuming, as well as expensive to the taxpayer. The family court, debated from the 1960s, *may* arrive, as promised from 2013.
    b. As for the civil courts, it might be more sensible to have one civil court, as considered by the Civil Justice Review 1988 and again, more recently, scrapping the division between county court and HC and scrapping the HC divisions. This would allow for more fluid distribution of work. Different ranks of judges could be retained, with work allocated to them according to its seriousness and complexity. Under the present system, many HC cases in the provinces are heard by "ticketed" circuit judges, demonstrating a considerable overlap and the falsity of the present HC/county court distinction.
    c. In the criminal courts, many trivial 'either way' cases are heard in the expensive Crown Court, because we are one of very few countries which gives the defendant the choice of trial court, so he can choose jury trial for stealing a bottle of milk. This right is very important to the English and Welsh but very expensive.
    d. On the other hand, unlike our common law daughter jurisdictions in North America, we do not allow the defendant to choose to be tried by judge alone in the Crown Court, instead of judge and jury. Auld L.J. found that in Canada and the USA many defendants opted for judge-alone trials. This would be much cheaper than jury trial and why deny the defendant the choice?
    e. There is no logic in who adjudicates in magistrates' courts. London's preference for professional magistrates (DJMCs) is an accident of history. Again, the defendant has no choice between a bench of three lay justices and a professional judge, because the court allocates the cases. Also, if we value collective decision making on guilt and

innocence and thus use 12 jurors or three magistrates, why do we allow any cases to be determined by a single DJMC?

f. While the civil appeal structure was reformed in the **Access to Justice Act 1999** so that an appropriate court and judge is used for each case, the criminal appeal structure is confusing, illogical and in need of reform, as demonstrated in Law Commission papers in 2007–2010.

5. Brief, concluding remarks, summarising the answer.

Civil Procedure

4

INTRODUCTION

1. Procedure in common law countries is *adversarial*. It is up to the parties to prepare their case, presenting relevant evidence and legal argument, unaided by the court. The judge is a neutral, non-interfering umpire.
2. The civil degree of proof is *on the balance of probabilities*, much lower than the criminal degree, *proof beyond reasonable doubt* so the court merely decides whether the claimant's case is more plausible than the defendant's case. Therefore, it is much easier to prove a civil case than a criminal one.
3. Generally, the claimant's aim is to satisfy the judge of the defendant's liability.
4. The state provides the civil courts to enable claimants to make use of the law against parties who have committed a civil wrong or threaten a civil wrong against them, such as a tort or breach of contract.
5. Unlike criminal cases, the state as a whole has no interest in the outcome, though elements of the state may be sued, such as a health authority.
6. Most civil disputes (well over 90 per cent) are settled between the parties, or their solicitors, by negotiation.
7. In the exceptional cases, where the aggrieved party goes to court, most are heard in the county court by a district judge (DJ) or, much less likely, a circuit judge (CJ). The High Court (HC) is reserved for special cases.
8. Trial is by judge alone, with rare exceptions in some torts, where a jury may be used to determine liability and damages. Some civil cases are heard in the magistrates' court and thus determined by lay magistrates or a district judge.
9. In this chapter we examine:

   - the Civil Procedure Rules (CPR) 1998, brought in as part of the "Woolf reforms";
   - their background;
   - evaluations of their success, and current reforms (the Jackson reforms); and
   - a description of the civil appeal procedure.

We also look at the procedure for referring a point of EU law to the Court of Justice of the EU, in a civil *or* criminal case. Note that the *trial* process, both civil and criminal, is examined in the chapter on criminal procedure.

CIVIL LITIGATION FROM 1999, FOLLOWING THE WOOLF REFORMS

The **CPR 1998** replaced two sets of rules for the High Court and county court in April 1999. They, and the Practice Directions (not law) accompanying them, embodied a radically different approach to civil procedure from the previous Dickensian litigation process and were modelled on recommendations by Lord Woolf in *Access to Justice* (1996), better known as the Woolf Report.

Civil Procedure Act 1997

Section 1 provides for one set of practice rules. Section 1(3) requires "that the civil justice system is accessible, fair and efficient". Section 2 provides for a Civil Court Rule Committee to include people "with experience in and knowledge of" consumer affairs and lay advice. Section 6 established a Civil Justice Council to keep the system under review, advise the Lord Chancellor (Minister of Justice) and suggest research.

KEY POINT

In the debate on the Civil Procedure Bill, this quotation from Lord Woolf illustrates frustration with the old system, long identified as being in need of reform:

> "When I set out on the inquiry which resulted in my report, I was very conscious that since 1885 there had already been over 60 reports, each urging reform of the civil justice system, yet the situation on which I had to report was one which many commentators described as being in crisis".

The Civil Procedure Rules 1998

The *overriding objective* is set out in r.1.1 (paraphrased):

The rules enable the court to deal with a case justly:

a. ensuring the parties are on an *equal footing*;
b. *saving expense*;
c. dealing with the case in a way which is *proportionate*:

to the amount of money involved
to the importance of the case
to the complexity of the issues
to the financial position of parties

d. ensuring that it is dealt with *expeditiously* and *fairly* and allotting to it an appropriate share of the court's *resources*; and
e. the court *must* apply the objective in interpreting the rules and exercising their powers. (My emphasis).

Pre-action protocols

These are statements of best practice in negotiation, encouraging exchange of information and putting the parties into a position to settle fairly. If they are ignored, the judge can punish the uncooperative party in costs, once the case comes to court. The pre-action stage is important because most people settle their disputes by negotiation. In 2009, a **Practice Direction** (not law) **on pre-action behaviour** attempted to strengthen the effects of protocols: The PD tries to help parties to settle so that proceedings do not have to be issued. It encourages early exchange of information and ADR. Parties MUST, for example:

- exchange information in reasonable time;
- disclose relevant documents;
- consider minimising cost of experts; and
- ATTEMPT ADR (though cannot be forced to do so).

KEY POINT

From 2009, as a matter of practice (not law), the court MUST take account of compliance with this PD and pre-action protocols when making directions.

Starting proceedings

The claimant (formerly plaintiff) or court issues and serves the claim on the defendant. This must include particulars of the claim (statement of case) or they must be served within four months. They may include points of law, witness lists and documents, and must include statements of truth and value and specify the remedy sought.

The defendant must, within 14 days:

- admit the claim;
- file a defence (statement of case); or
- acknowledge.

If not, the claimant may request a *default judgment* (Pt 12). This means asking the court to grant his claim as the defendant has not entered a defence. *Most cases end at this point.* The defendant may issue a claim against a co-defendant or third party or make a *counterclaim* (Pt 20). The claimant may reply and defend. The parties may write direct to others requesting further information.

Allocation

Defended claims (i.e. the exceptions) are allocated to one of three tracks once the defendant has completed the pre-trial checklist.

- Small claims track for most actions under £5,000, except housing possession and personal injury, where the limit is £1,000. Higher value claims may be allocated to this track by consent.
- Fast track for most cases £5–25,000, which can be tried in a day. Oral expert evidence is limited to two fields and one expert per field.
- Multi-track for claims over £25,000 or over one day's trial.

Claims with no monetary value are allocated where the judge considers they will be dealt with most justly. The judge may transfer a case to another court. **Note**: The monetary limits in the small claims and fast tracks may be raised during the lifetime of this book, in the Jackson reforms, explained below.

Discretionary factors

The procedural judge must have regard to:

- the nature of the remedy sought;
- the complexity of facts, law and evidence;
- the number of parties;
- the value of the counterclaim;
- whether there will be oral evidence;
- the importance of the claim to non-parties;
- the parties' views; and
- the circumstances of the parties.

The Woolf Report suggested the following cases for the multi-track:

- those of public importance;
- test cases;
- medical negligence cases (now "clinical disputes"); and
- cases with the right to jury trial.

District judges (DJs) have unlimited jurisdiction to assess damages, unless otherwise directed.

The court's duty to manage cases

This had already been introduced from 1994 in Practice Directions, including timetabling, the requirement for skeleton arguments and limitation of oral argument. The *duty* now includes:

- encouraging parties to co-operate;
- identifying issues at an early stage;
- deciding promptly which issues can be disposed of summarily;
- deciding the order of issues;
- encouraging Alternative Dispute Resolution (ADR);
- helping parties settle;
- fixing timetables;
- considering cost benefit (of every element of the case);
- grouping issues;
- dealing with a case in the absence of one or more parties;
- making use of IT; and
- directing the trial process quickly and efficiently.

Sanctions for failure to comply include striking out, costs and debarring part of a case or evidence. Trials will only be postponed as a last resort. Most cases are managed by county court DJs. HC masters manage most cases in the Royal Courts of Justice, except commercial cases. The court controls what evidence it is prepared to hear and the format in which it is prepared to hear witnesses.

Interim orders

The parties may apply for the orders listed below but this should be unnecessary in many cases because the judge's case management powers allow her to act on her own initiative. Hearings may be by telephone.

- Pre-action remedies if urgent;
- applications without notice (formerly called *ex parte*);
- extensions or shortening of time;
- requiring attendance;
- separating or consolidating or excluding issues;
- deciding the order of issues;
- staying (pausing) all or part of the case, hoping for settlement;
- interim injunctions/declarations;
- freezing injunctions and search orders;

- pre-action disclosure (formerly discovery) or inspection; and
- interim payments and offers to settle.

Summary judgment

This may be initiated by the claimant, defendant or court, where the claim or defence *"has no real prospect of success"*. The court may enter judgment, dismiss the case, strike out a claim, or make a conditional order.

Expert witnesses

Lord Woolf felt that over-use of experts had made litigation costly and unduly adversarial. The assumption now is that one witness will suffice or, if more than one is permitted, that they will agree a statement pre-trial. Under Pt 35, their duty is to help the court and no party may call an expert or use a report without the court's permission.

Small claims procedure

Hearings are in public (as required by the **European Convention on HR**) but are normally held in the DJ's chambers. She may adopt any procedure she considers fair, including hearing lay representatives. Appeal lies to a circuit judge (CJ) on law or serious irregularity. Costs are fixed at low levels.

Fast-track procedure

The intention was for the court to maintain *proportionality*, which means limiting the costs recoverable from the unsuccessful party. The aim was to increase access to justice by removing uncertainty and obtaining a speedy result. The court directs the timetable and fixes the trial date no more than 30 weeks ahead. The intention was to provide little scope for either party to create extra work to gain a tactical advantage. Lord Woolf said it was important for the court to protect the weaker party against oppressive or unreasonable behaviour by a powerful party. Standard directions now include disclosure, the exchange of witness statements, expert evidence and fixing the trial date. Parties are encouraged to use a single expert. The standard timetable is nine months from the issue of proceedings to trial. A document bundle must be produced to the court three to seven days pre-trial and may include an agreed case summary. Trial costs are meant to be kept *proportionate* to the amount recovered. (As is explained below, this aim has not succeeded). Other costs are assessed "summarily" by the judge after the trial.

Multi-track procedure

This varies. Simple cases are treated like fast track ones. Complex ones may have several directions hearings:

- a case management conference, which may be by telephone;
- a pre-trial review of the statement of issues; and
- other directions hearings.

Disclosure

Lord Woolf thought uncontrolled discovery (now disclosure) was a major generator of cost. Now, standard disclosure requires only documents on which a party relies and documents which:

- adversely affect his case;
- adversely affect another party's case;
- support another party's case; and
- those required by a Practice Direction.

The court's power to control evidence

The court has power to control the delivery of evidence and whether it is prepared to hear oral, hearsay or written evidence, etc.

Offers to settle (Part 36)

This procedure encourages the parties to settle by financial incentive. Under the old rules the defendant could make a payment into court and force the plaintiff to take a gamble: take the money or proceed to trial and risk paying both sides' costs since the time of the payment in. The intention of the new rules is that allowing the claimant to make an offer to settle alters the balance of power. The judge knows nothing of the offer to settle. (See also Part 2 of the **Legal Aid, Sentencing and Punishment of Offenders (LASPO) Act 2012**).

Wasted costs

The court may make a wasted costs order against a representative if he has acted improperly, unreasonably or negligently, and his conduct has caused unnecessary costs to the other party.

General points

The reforms were intended to cut the length of trial. Suitable cases may be disposed without a hearing (r.1.4 (2)). The statutory right to jury trial was unaffected in deceit, libel, slander, malicious prosecution and false imprisonment. Generally, hearings must be in open court, under art.6 of the **European Convention on Human Rights.** There are exceptions where hearings may be in private, such as a case involving a child. Witness statements count as evidence-in-chief so if you bring a witness, you may not examine her in court if she has already made a statement. Supplementary questions may be asked only for "good reason".

The right to know the case against you

This point has nothing to do with the civil procedure rules: at common law, you have the right to know the case against you, under the rules of natural justice. The court has no power to adopt a closed material procedure in an ordinary civil case: *Al-Rawi v Security Service* [2011] UKSC 34.

The Woolf Reforms and Alternative Dispute Resolution

Lord Woolf was keen to promote ADR. Under r.1.4 of the CPR, the court is under a duty to encourage ADR, where appropriate. The courts have been instrumental in promoting ADR, by providing the facilities for it and by penalising parties who refuse to cooperate. See next chapter.

BACKGROUND TO THE "WOOLF REFORMS"

English civil procedure was notoriously adversarial and referred to in terms of a battle or game. Until the 1980s, the parties "kept their cards close to the chest", pre-trial, and it was difficult to assess the strength of the opposition's case. This led to a number of problems which were depicted in the literature of Charles Dickens and identified and discussed in over 60 reports in the twentieth century. Some of the problems were:

Delay

This was caused by one or both parties manipulating the pre-trial stages for their own ends. It was in the defendant's interests to delay being ordered to pay damages as long as possible. High Court (HC) cases took years. The length of trial was dictated by the behaviour of the parties and the case they chose to present, with the court out of control.

Inequality of the parties

A battle is only fair if the parties are of equal strength. In most cases, one party is more powerful, in terms of money, other resources or information. This is obvious where a consumer is suing a large corporation or where someone who had suffered negligent surgery is suing a health authority. This inequality allowed the powerful party to dominate the other into submission and, since most cases are settled out of court, it was thought that they often settled on terms more acceptable to the powerful party.

consultation process in 2010–12 but they are banned in claims for personal injury or death by s.56 of the **LASPO Act** (effective April 2013) and the Minister may ban them in other cases.]

6. There should be fixed costs in the fast track. [By 2012, nothing has happened.]
7. A Costs Council should annually review lawyers' rates and fixed costs.
8. Lawyers should be permitted to enter into contingency fee agreements taking a percentage of damages won by the claimant. These were legal in Scotland and the US but always viewed with disdain in England because they were thought to encourage "ambulance chasing". [Section 45 of the **LASPO Act** permits these "damages based agreements" between lawyer and client in cases where a "no win-no-fee" contract is permissible. In October 2012, Ministers announced that damages-based agreements will be permitted in all areas of civil litigation, with a 50 per cent cap, and a 25 per cent cap in personal injury cases.]
9. Legal expenses insurance should be promoted, for instance, as part of house insurance.
10. ADR should be promoted.
11. Lawyers and judges should be trained in costs management. [See 1.]
12. Expert witnesses should be examined concurrently in court, known as "hot tubbing". [See M. Solon at 162 (2012) N.L.J. 874].

In 2011, the Minister of Justice also launched a consultation, *Solving disputes in the county courts: creating a simpler, quicker and more proportionate system*. Re-emphasising proportionality, it proposed raising the small claims limit to £15,000. The HC would be limited to cases over £100,000 and housing equity cases over £300,000. All small claimants would be required to have attempted mediation. The government response is on the Ministry website.

CIVIL APPEALS

Appeals from magistrates' courts

In family matters appeal lies to the county court on the grounds that the decision is wrong in law or in excess of jurisdiction.

Appeals from the county court and HC from 2000

The procedure is contained in the **Access to Justice Act 1999**, in the **CPR 1998** and other rules and Practice Directions. The regime is explained by the CA (Civil Division) in *Tanfern Ltd v Cameron-MacDonald* [2000] 1 W.L.R. 1311. The Labour Government planned to achieve its objectives of *proportionality* and *efficiency* by "diverting from the Court of Appeal those cases which, by their nature, do not require the attention of the most senior judges in the country" (*Modernising Justice*, 1998). The principles are as follows:

- Permission to appeal will only be given where the court considers that an appeal would have a *real prospect of success*.
- In normal circumstances more than one appeal cannot be justified.
- There should be no automatic right to appeal.

Jurisdiction

- In fast-track cases heard by a DJ, appeal lies to a CJ.
- In those heard by a CJ, appeal lies to a HC judge.
- In multi-track cases, all appeals against final orders lie to the CA.
- Exceptional cases involving important points of principle, or which affect a number of litigants, may go straight to the CA.

Composition

Changes to the composition, procedures and management of the CA were designed to help it operate more efficiently. Under the **1999 Act**, the CA can consist of any number of judges, one to five, according to the importance and complexity of the case.

Approach

Generally, every appeal is limited to a review of the decision of the lower court, unless a Practice Direction provides otherwise, or the court considers that it would be in the interests of justice to hold a rehearing.

Grounds

The appeal court will only allow an appeal where the lower court was wrong (in substance) or where it was unjust because of a serious procedural or other irregularity. The decision of the lower court attracts a much greater significance than pre-2000.

Powers

Generally, an appeal court has all the powers of the lower court. It also has the power to affirm, set aside or vary any order or judgment of the lower court, to refer any claim or issue for determination by the lower court, to order a new trial or hearing, and to make a costs order.

Second appeals

Second appeals would now be a rarity. The decision of the first appeal court should be given primacy, unless the CA itself considered that the appeal would raise an important point of principle or practice or that there was some other compelling reason for it to hear a second appeal.

Appeals from the CA to the UKSC

An application for permission must be made first to the CA and, if refused, may be made to the UKSC. Appeals are normally heard by five UKSC justices (though increasingly, by nine). The parties must each lodge a printed "case", a succinct statement of the arguments below, and of the issues before the Court. Judgment is normally reserved.

FURTHER READING

Darbyshire on the ELS (2011), Chapter 10, material referred to therein and web updates.
Civil Procedure Rules and Practice Directions; press releases, Ministry of Justice website.
Civil Justice Council website.
Civil Justice Quarterly
Judges' speeches, Judiciary website

REFERENCES TO THE COURT OF JUSTICE OF THE EU REQUESTING A PRELIMINARY RULING

Queries on the interpretation of a point of EU law can be sent up to the Court of Justice of the EU from a civil or criminal case at any point in the procedure. Article 267 of the Treaty on the Functioning of the EU concerns references to the Court by domestic courts of Member States:

> "The Court of Justice of the European Union shall have jurisdiction to give preliminary rulings concerning:
>
> (a) the interpretation of this Treaty;
> (b) the validity and interpretation of acts of the institutions, bodies, offices or agencies of the Union;
>
> Where such a question is raised before any court or tribunal of a Member State, that court or tribunal may, if it considers that a decision on the question is necessary to enable it to give judgment, request the Court to give a ruling thereon.

Where any such question is raised in a case pending before a court or tribunal of a Member State against whose decisions there is no judicial remedy under national law, that court or tribunal shall bring the matter before the Court...."

Points to note:

1. Any judicial or quasi-judicial body may refer, however lowly. For instance, magistrates' courts and tribunals.
2. The "question" may be raised by the parties or the court but only the court may make the reference.
3. The ruling is preliminary only in the sense that the case then goes back to the original court for it to apply the law to the facts. The Court of Justice's rulings on EU law are final.
4. The Court will not answer hypothetical questions.
5. Facts should normally be found before reference.
6. The Court has accepted the doctrine of *acte clair*. This means that a point need not be referred if it is "reasonably clear and free from doubt".
7. References are discretionary, except where there is no judicial remedy against the domestic court's decision. In that instance, an obligation to refer arises.
8. The case in the English or Welsh court is suspended, while the procedure is completed but it takes an average of two years for the Court to answer the question sent over, thus causing immense delay.

FURTHER READING

Darbyshire on the ELS (2011), Chapter 3.
Court of Justice of the EU website.

Revision Checklist

You should now know and understand:

- **why common law procedure is called adversarial;**
- **how civil cases are distributed between courts;**
- **civil procedure under the CPR 1998, in outline, including the overriding objective and the importance of pre-action protocols;**
- **the background to the Woolf reforms;**

- **research and commentary evaluating their success;**
- **Lord Justice Jackson's 2009 recommendations and their outcomes;**
- **basic civil appeal procedure; and**
- **the art.267 procedure for referring questions of EU law to the Court of Justice of the EU.**

QUESTION AND ANSWER

The Question

Explain and critically evaluate "the Woolf reforms" to civil procedure.

Advice and the Answer

Advice

"Explain" means describe the main points, in outline, and explore the reasons why the Woolf reforms were executed. "Critically evaluate", does not mean you have to say something critical about the reforms. Criticism means the same as theatre criticism, which also includes praise and neutral assessment.

Answer guide

1. Explain what is meant by "the Woolf reforms", outlining the main points of the post-1999 regime and remembering to mention case management and the overriding objective of the **CPR 1998**.
2. Explain why civil procedure was reformed, by briefly outlining the main problems identified by Lord Woolf in *Access to Justice*, 1996.
3. Examine critiques of the Woolf reforms outlined in this chapter, ELS textbooks, the Civil Justice Council website and journals such as the *Civil Justice Quarterly*, *Legal Action*, *New Law Journal* and so on. Pay attention to critiques published in journals and newspapers in 2009 as that was the tenth anniversary of the **CPR**. Look for commentary on the Jackson Report, responses to the Government consultations on his recommendations and commentary on the **LASPO Bill/Act 2012**. Look out for further legislation such as rules changing the small claims and fast track limits.

TRIBUNAL STRUCTURE 2010

UK UPPER TRUBUNAL			
Senior President (L.J.) and Deputy (HC judge)			
Immigration & Asylum Chamber	Lands Chamber	Administrative Appeals Chamber	Tax & Chancery Chamber
Immigration and asylum appeals	Jurisdiction formerly exercised by the Lands Tribunal (land appeals)	Appeals from the chambers below, on points of law; judicial review of criminal injuries comp; appeals from Traffic Commissioners; appeals from the General Regulatory Chamber.	Appeals from Tax & Duties Chamber; charity appeals; pension regulation; financial services.
President, Vice President (HC judges), other HC judges, circuit judges, UT immigration judges	President, Vice President, (HC judges), other HC judges, circuit judges, UT judges	President, VP, HC judges, circuit judges, UT judges	President, VP, HC and circuit chancery judges, Upper Tribunal judges, non-legal members

Appeals on point of law or judicial review

FIRST TIER TRIBUNAL					
Immigration & Asylum Chamber	War Pensions & Armed Forces Compensation Chamber	Social Entitlement Chamber	Health, Education & Social Care Chamber	General Regulatory Chamber	Tax & Duties Chamber
Immigration and asylum	War pensions and armed forces compensation	Asylum support; social security and child support; criminal injuries compensation; housing benefit; council tax benefit, etc.	Care standards; mental health review; special educational needs and disability; family health services appeals.	Charities; consumer credit appeals; estate agents; transport; gambling; claims management services; information appeals; immigration services.	Tax, VAT and duties.
President, Deputies (circuit judges), First Tier immigration judges, non-legal members	President, Deputies (circuit judges),First Tier tribunal judges, members of armed forces	President, Deputies, First Tier tribunal judges	President, Deputies, lay members, doctors, psychiatrists, etc.	President, etc.	President, non-legal members, etc.

Employment Appeal Tribunal
Employment Appeals
President (High Court judge), HC and circuit judges, employment judges, non-legal members

Employment Tribunals
Unfair dismissal; redundancy; discrimination, etc.
Employment judges and non-legal members

Employment is not part of the new structure.

Most first instance appeals will be heard in the First Tier Tribunal. The Upper Tribunal is a Superior Court of Record, like the High Court. Appeals from the UT on important points of law lie to the Court of Appeal. Non-legal members sit in some UT and some FTT cases (in accordance with the tribunals they replaced). Court of Appeal judges may sit in the UT.

Alternatives to the Civil Courts

5

INTRODUCTION

In the nineteenth and twentieth centuries, some alternative forums to the civil courts were established.

- Tribunals: Parliament has legislated to allocate some disputes to them, mainly appeals against state decisions.
- Arbitration: speedy private dispute resolution, invented in the industrial revolution. Awards are legally binding and arbitration is regulated by the Arbitration Act 1996.
- ADR (alternative dispute resolution): all the other types of private dispute resolution, developed since the 1970s, mainly informal but some are statutory.

KEY POINT

While the litigant may choose to take a dispute to arbitration or use ADR, they **cannot choose to go to a tribunal**. Parliament made the choice in the many Acts creating tribunals.

TRIBUNALS

What are tribunals and how do they compare with courts?

Until 2009, tribunals were too disparate to be described as a "system", though the main ones are being restructured, following the Tribunals, Courts and Enforcement Act 2007. There were over 100 sets of tribunals, each highly specialised, dealing with only one area of the law. Most deal with disputes between the citizen and the state, for instance, over tax, state benefits, school allocation and so on. Others, such as employment tribunals, adjudicate between private parties. Some tribunals form a nationwide network, such as the new Social Entitlement Chamber, whilst others are one central unit.

Why did over 100 sets of tribunals develop alongside, but outside, the court system?

Most were created in the twentieth century. As the welfare state grew, they were developed to adjudicate between citizen and state because the Labour and Liberal Governments which developed state power distrusted the (then Conservative) judiciary. The Franks Committee was established to examine concern over this bureaucratisation, and reported, in 1957, that tribunals should be seen as performing a judicial, not an executive, function and they should be better regulated. They identified four main reasons for their popularity:

- cheapness (no formal buildings or judicial regalia, or court fees);
- accessibility and speed;
- freedom from technicality so people could represent themselves; and
- expert knowledge (of the panel).

Criticisms

- They were separate and administered separately. This was confusing, inefficient and wasteful.
- Some had become so court-like that the litigant struggled without a lawyer, yet legal aid was not, and is still not, available before most tribunals. For example, lawyers often represent appellants before the Employment Appeal Tribunal on a voluntary basis, because employment law is very complex. Unrepresented parties cause problems for the tribunal panel. Research demonstrates that representation by *anyone* enhances the applicant's chances of success.
- Some now have bigger delays than the courts.
- Some are so court-like, with complexity and delay, that they have lost any advantage over the courts. Applicants are encouraged to use ADR.
- Lack of visibility.
- Informality can lead to a lack of due process.
- See further Leggatt below.

The Leggatt Report

A review by Sir Andrew Leggatt was published in 2001: *Tribunals for Users-One System, One Service*. Below are the main points.

- It concentrated on the 70 bodies providing specialist adjudication which would otherwise be dealt with by the courts.
- It suggested that tribunals should be used instead of courts: where users could present their own cases; where expertise was a major

issue; and where a tribunal could effectively deal with issues of mixed fact and law.

- Problems were: isolation leading to duplication of effort; lack of resources and IT; and delays and poor communication with users.
- Some tribunal members felt they could not be seen as independent of the government departments administering them.
- Leggatt rejected creating a separate system of administrative courts as exists in European legal systems.
- Independence could only be assured by separating tribunals from government departments and forming them into a coherent system, directed by a board and administered by a Tribunals Service and the Department of Constitutional Affairs ("DCA") (now Ministry of Justice).
- The civil justice reforms should be applied to tribunal procedure.
- Confusing overlaps with court jurisdiction should be removed.
- The tribunals system should be divided by subject-matter into eight subject sections, with a single appellate division in each.
- Judicial review should be excluded. Appeals on law should go to the CA.
- Tribunal members should be trained by the Judicial Studies Board (now Judicial College) in interpersonal skills.
- A Judicial Appointments Commissioner should supervise appointments.
- Government departments should consider introducing internal review procedures to ensure that their case is correct in fact and law, and that opposing the citizen's appeal was a justifiable use of public funds. They should disseminate lessons learned from tribunals.

Government response

They started implementing these recommendations before Leggatt reported. In 2002, the Law Commission set out plans for reforming the eight tribunals for resolving land, valuation and housing disputes. This follows the recommendation for a clearer structure for users without overlaps. In 2006, a new unified Tribunals Service came into operation and has now been amalgamated with the Court Service to form Her Majesty's Courts and Tribunals Service.

In 2004, Government published a White Paper (document containing plans for legislation), *Transforming Public Services: Complaints, Redress and Tribunals*. It examined not just tribunals but the whole administrative justice system and dispute resolution process, with the aim of "helping to improve standards of decision making" and providing better redress where things go wrong, to divert cases from tribunals. Tribunal panel chairmen were renamed tribunal judges. The **Tribunals, Courts and Enforcement Act 2007** provides a Senior President (a Lord Justice of Appeal, the first being appointed in 2005), heading a "simplified statutory framework" to provide more coherence, organised as in the diagram from 2009–10. It replaced the Council on Tribunals, created in 1957, with an Administrative Justice and Tribunals Council with a broader remit. The Coalition Government is currently threatening to abolish it though a Parliamentary select committee urged them not to do so in 2012. To abolish it would, I suggest, be a retrograde step, taking us back to the 1956 situation.

Tribunal Members

Chairmen of tribunals, now usually called tribunal judges, are normally members of the legal profession, sitting as part-timers. Lawyer-chairmen were favoured by the Franks Committee in 1957. As a result of the **Constitutional Reform Act 2005**, from 2006 tribunal judges are appointed by the L.C. following selection competitions run by the Judicial Appointments Commission.

The two "wingers" who sit with the tribunal judge are usually not legally qualified but are selected for their expertise. For example, employment tribunal and employment appeal tribunal members are usually drawn from employers' and employees' organisations; those tribunals concerned with the collection of revenue often appoint accountants, and so on. In 2009, there were about 8,000 non-lawyers who sat on tribunals. The Government has been criticised for abolishing lay involvement in some tribunals, in the late 1990s, notably social security tribunals. Tribunal training is undertaken by the Judicial College.

ARBITRATION

Arbitration is the commercial world's alternative to slow, expensive and inconvenient HC litigation. It means the adjudication of a dispute, usually by an individual expert in the subject-matter involved, or a lawyer. It is more formal than ADR and results in a legally binding decision. Arbitration is regulated by the **Arbitration Act 1996**. The arbitrator will normally follow the same stages as civil litigation but submissions are often written and hearings may be by telephone. Most arbitral rules permit the arbitrator to act inquisitorially, that is, asking questions. She is not bound by strict rules of evidence or substantive law so, if the parties agree, she can decide according to equity and good conscience. She gives a reasoned decision, enforceable in court. An award may be challenged in court for three reasons:

- Jurisdiction;
- a point of law of general public importance; or
- a serious irregularity.

The Act has been subject to a lot of interpretation. In *Warborough Investments Ltd v S. Robinson & Sons (Holdings) Ltd* [2003] EWCA Civ 751, the CA held that, under s.1, the courts were required to accord to arbitrators a reasonably wide discretion.

Arbitration may arise in one of three ways:

By contract The parties may have entered a contract, in some context such as shipping or insurance, and, in a clause, they have agreed to refer any disputes arising under the contract to an arbitrator (who may be named in the contract). This is significant, not just because it is common trade practice, but also because lay people are often, unwittingly, parties to an arbitration clause. For instance, almost all insurance policies contain an arbitration clause BUT where a business contracts with a consumer, they must fully explain any arbitration clause and an arbitration clause will automatically be deemed unfair where disputes are for less than £5,000, under delegated legislation, confirmed in *Mylcrist Builders v Buck* [2008] EWHC 2172 (TCC). If one of the parties tries to ignore such a clause and goes to court, the court may order a "stay" (a stop) of proceedings so that the matter may be referred to arbitration BUT In *Allianz SpA and Another v West Tankers Inc* Case C-185/07, 2009, the ECJ ruled that a court in one EU Member State had no power to rule that a party should drop a case in another EU state on the ground that the parties had agreed to refer any dispute to arbitration. Under **Regulation 44/2001**, the Member State's court had the exclusive power to rule on its own jurisdiction.

By reference from the court A judge in the Commercial Court may refer a dispute to an arbitrator.

By agreement Once a dispute has arisen, the parties may choose to go to an arbitrator rather than a court, in same way that they may choose ADR, below.

Background

The rise of arbitration occurred in the late-nineteenth century when trade associations wished to have their disputes privately, cheaply and speedily resolved by experts, for instance, construction disputes involving Britain's new railway network, or arguments about liability for a ship's rotting cargo. London is an important international arbitration centre, always worried about losing its market-share to other international arbitration centres, such as Paris, Singapore, New York etc. A closely related procedure is "adjudication", used in the construction industry, where an adjudicator is expected to make a swift decision.

Advantages

- speed;
- privacy, important where commercial, sensitive information is involved;
- finality;
- expertise—the arbitrator will be an expert and some are also lawyers;
- low cost (the parties pay privately for the arbitrator);
- the International Convention on the Recognition and Enforcement of Foreign Arbitral Awards obliges contracting states to recognise foreign arbitral awards; and
- unlike ADR, the decision is final and binding, the arbitrator is regulated by the **1996 Act** and parties can appeal to the courts.

Advantages of London in international arbitrations

- Use of English law: many international contracts stipulate that English law governs the contract.
- London's financial and commercial power.
- Position in international time zones.
- Historically, it is an international maritime and insurance centre and international law firms use London as a springboard into Europe.

Disadvantages

- It has become lawyer-dominated and can be expensive.
- Appeal to the courts is possible in England so this destroys finality.
- We are subject to international criticism that our courts interfere too much. In *Lesotho Highlands Development Authority v Impregilo SpA* [2005] UKHL 43, the House of Lords (law lords) reminded us that the philosophy of the **1996 Act** was to drastically reduce the extent of court intervention.
- Practitioners may prefer to arbitrate in Paris because of our labour-intensive, expensive emphasis on document disclosure, longer hearings, the cultural arrogance of English lawyers, convinced their methods are superior, and the use of barristers and judges as arbitrators who attempt to replicate court procedure. (See interviews in an article by Smulian, Law Society's *Gazette*, June 19, 2003).

ALTERNATIVE DISPUTE RESOLUTION (ADR)

The phrase was imported from the US in about 1990 but mediation was being developed in England and Wales from the 1970s. Lord Chancellors Mackay and Irvine (1980–2003) took an active interest in ADR, as a means of avoiding the public and private expense and the private pain of litigation. Since the mid-1990s, civil advocates have been required to inform their clients of ADR (It is now a requirement of the **Civil Procedure Rules 1998** r.1). There are three main categories: mediation; conciliation; and arbitration (above). Schemes may be private or court-linked.

Mediation

This is the least formal. The parties voluntarily refer their dispute to an independent third party who will discuss the issues with both sides and, by acting as a "go-between", will assist them to discuss and negotiate areas of conflict and identify and settle certain issues. It will only be successful if parties are willing to compromise. It is not appropriate for disputes where there is little room for compromise such as housing possession proceedings.

Conciliation

This lies midway between informal mediation and formal arbitration. The process is very similar to mediation but the third party may offer a non-binding opinion which may lead to a settlement.

Other types are self-explanatory

They include early neutral evaluation, expert determination, mini-trial by a privately hired judge, expert determination and online dispute resolution.

Note: ADR is not suitable where the parties want a court to clarify the law or where only a court order will do, e.g. an injunction to prevent a threatened breach of the law.

Examples of use of ADR

- The best known mediation schemes are those offered to family disputants. Thousands of people, notably solicitors, were trained as mediators to satisfy the mediation requirements of the Family Law Act 1996. Public funding can be obtained for it. Since 2002, unless inappropriate, solicitors are required to explain mediation and collaboration to clients. By 2005, over 250 lawyers had been trained in "collaborative law", a no-court, non-adversarial scheme originating in the USA. The government and courts strongly encourage family mediation and in-court conciliation, but research reached mixed conclusions on success

(L. Trinder and J. Kellett MoJ Research Report 15/07, MoJ website). It is not appropriate where violence has been alleged or where drug/alcohol abuse is involved. Under a Family Procedure Rules 2010 pre-action protocol, since 2011, parties applying for some court orders are required to attend an information meeting and, in 2011, the Government announced that anyone wishing to contest the terms of a divorce must attend a mediation awareness session. National Audit Office figures on legally aided mediation showed that the average length of a mediated case was 110 days instead of 435 days in court. The cost per client was £535 instead of £2,800.

- Welsh NHS trusts piloted mediation in clinical negligence disputes and it was copied in England in the NHS Redress Scheme. Even a multi-million pound damages action for birth injuries cost only about £10,000 to mediate, whereas it might cost £150,000 to litigate in the civil courts. Lord Justice Jackson, in his 2009 final report, expressed concern over the huge cost of clinical negligence to the National Health Service.
- The government announced in 2001 that it would be using ADR in its disputes. It saved £6 million in 2002–03. Departments now include ADR clauses in their standard procurement contracts.
- The Technology & Construction Court introduced a court settlement process. Parties may request the help of specially trained judges.
- In 2005, the Government launched a national mediation helpline to put callers in touch with an accredited mediator.
- From 2013, employment tribunal fees will be tailored to encourage people to settle or mediate rather than take their case to a tribunal.
- Directive 2008/52/EC encourages the use of mediation in cross-border disputes. It obliges EU Member States to encourage training and gives every judge the right to suggest mediation.

Will the courts enforce ADR?

- The Commercial Court has always been very keen to divert part or the whole of a case to ADR or arbitration. Coleman J. enforced a mediation clause in a commercial contract in *Cable & Wireless PLC v IBM UK Ltd* [2002] EWHC 2059.
- The CA has been equally keen. In the leading case of *Dunnett v Railtrack* [2002] EWCA Civ 303, they held that where a party refused to cooperate in ADR they might be penalised in costs. As a result of this, statistics published by the Centre for Effective Dispute Resolution (CEDR) showed an increase in ADR.
- The courts backtracked, in *Halsey v Milton Keynes General NHS Trust* [2004] EWCA 576, holding that compulsion would be a breach of art.6

(fair trial) of the **European Convention on Human Rights** because it constrained access to the courts.

- In a 2008 speech, the Master of the Rolls acknowledged that *Halsey* might have been over-cautious. Compulsory ADR did not breach art.6 and was indeed referred to in the **EC Directive on Mediation**. Compulsory mediation had been introduced in a number of US jurisdictions.
- Many courts have established court-based mediation schemes and renamed themselves Civil Justice Centres. Following an unsuccessful mediation experiment in 1996, the Central London County Court renamed itself and in 2004 started a scheme of random referral. Manchester County Court renamed itself Manchester Civil Justice Centre. The Small Claims Mediation Service is attached to some courts. Some cases are referred to a national helpline and then directed to mediators accredited by the Civil Mediation Council. As explained in the previous chapter, a 2011 MoJ consultation paper suggested referring all small claimants to attempt mediation.
- See further, on compulsion: M. Ahmed (2012) 31(2) C.J.Q. 151.

Attitudes to ADR

- Generally, judges were quick to latch on to ADR and strongly promoted it from about 1990 but lawyers were slow to accept it. There was very low uptake. In the Central London County Court 1996 scheme only five per cent of parties agreed to ADR, research by Genn demonstrating widespread ignorance by lawyers and fear of showing weakness. In 1998–99, parties in only 12 of 250 CA cases accepted ADR. Take-up of the Commercial Court's ADR scheme was "modest" in 1996–2000 (all researched by Genn).
- A big boost came from r.1 of the **CPR 1998** and a critical core of big law firms started offering it.
- Another breakthrough came when the Law Society and ADR Group successfully challenged in court the refusal of legal aid for non-family ADR.
- The Centre for Effective Dispute Resolution audits the use of ADR. The 2012 audit claimed that there had been a 15 per cent increase in civil and commercial mediation in each of the previous two years. More than 70 per cent of mediations settle on the day.
- The family lawyers' group Resolution said the use of collaborative law in divorce proceedings had increased by 87 per cent in 2006–7.
- In her 2008 Hamlyn lectures, *Judging Civil Justice* (Cambridge, 2009), Genn argued forcefully that anti-litigation pressure, especially from judges, had already gone too far
- But see two interesting articles by P. Randolph who said "mandatory

ADR is accepted globally": (2010) 160 N.L.J. 499 and (2011) 161 N.L.J. 207.

Revision Checklist

You should now know and understand:

- **why tribunals grew up outside the court system, what issues they deal with, and how they were thought to be better for the litigant;**
- **the criticisms that were made, prompting the Leggatt Review;**
- **Leggatt's recommendations and how these translated into the 2007 Act and the structure in the diagram;**
- **that unlike ADR and arbitration, a party cannot choose to go to a tribunal;**
- **what arbitration is, why it developed, how it differs from ADR (statutory regulation and enforcement by and appeal to the courts) and its advantages and disadvantages; and**
- **what is meant by ADR (with examples), why and how the courts and Government are keen to promote it (advantages over litigation) and how it has developed since 1990.**

FURTHER READING/UPDATING

Darbyshire on the ELS, 2011, Chapter 11, materials listed therein and web updates.
Civil Justice Quarterly
New Law Journal
Public Law

Websites

Administrative Justice and Tribunals Council (including comprehensive summary of academic and research papers)
CEDR (on ADR)
Chartered Institute of Arbitrators
HM Courts and Tribunals Service
Judiciary (judges' speeches)
Leggatt Review
Ministry of Justice

QUESTION AND ANSWER

The Question

Give an account of the development of ADR in England and Wales and explore the reasons for its rise in popularity.

Advice and the Answer

Advice

Do not get distracted into describing types of ADR at any length. This is such simple information that it does not demonstrate intelligence or analytical skill or real understanding.

Answer guide

1. *Briefly* explain what is meant by ADR and give examples. Your textbook will provide this information. There is no need to resort to dictionary definitions or Wikipedia.
2. "Give an account of" means tell the story of. This story is explained at greater length in *Darbyshire on the ELS* (2011).
3. Explain the advantages of ADR, especially cheapness, speed and informality.
4. Explain how ADR was generally imported from the US and was promoted by Lord Chancellors Irvine and Mackay in their policies and speeches.
5. Explain how it has been emphasised in the **Civil Procedure Rules 1998** since 1999 and promoted by the Government in its litigation.
6. Explain how it has been promoted through court-annexed schemes and how the CA have promoted it by penalising litigants who have persisted in civil litigation rather than considering ADR (*Dunnett v Railtrack*, etc.).
7. Explain how it has been promoted by making public funding (legal aid) available for use in ADR such as mediation.
8. Mention that research demonstrated lawyers' initial reluctance to use ADR.
9. Read and cite articles and statistics from the CEDR website, which is one of the best sources of material evaluating the popularity of ADR at your time of writing and over the previous years.

10. Check the Civil Justice Council website for research on ADR and annual reports.
11. In your conclusion, briefly outline what you have just said.

Criminal Procedure

6

INTRODUCTION

In common law systems, criminal procedure, like civil procedure, is adversarial, with prosecution and defence responsible for adducing evidence and bringing legal argument to establish their case. (The **European Convention on Human Rights** also requires that criminal proceedings are adversarial). The court is not involved in directing investigations. While civil procedure is straightforward, criminal procedure is much more complex. It has been bedevilled by constant changes in recent years, as each Home Secretary tries to demonstrate how "tough on crime" he is, promoting layer upon layer of criminal justice legislation, which is very difficult for the courts to apply and lawyers to understand, let alone the public. In this chapter we will examine the following.

- The fundamental rules of criminal procedure, deriving from the common law, the **European Convention on Human Rights 1950** and the Criminal Procedure Rules.
- Pre-trial criminal procedure.
- The trial process, both criminal and civil.
- The appeal process.
- The post-appeal process for re-examining alleged miscarriages of justice.

BACKGROUND: REFORM BODIES

In 1990–91, faith in the criminal process plummeted, with the acknowledgment by the Court of Appeal (Criminal Division) (CACD) of a number of miscarriages of justice which had resulted in many innocent people spending decades in gaol. The most notable were the Guildford Four, the Maguires and the Birmingham Six. In 1991, the Home Secretary appointed a Royal Commission on Criminal Justice (RCCJ), which reported in 1993. Its terms of reference were to examine the effectiveness of the criminal process in securing the conviction of the guilty and the acquittal of the innocent. Its recommendations were heavily criticised since many bolstered the power of prosecutors. In 1997, the Home Secretary received a *Review of Delay in the Criminal Justice System*, better known as the Narey Report. Many of Narey's recommendations were enacted in the Crime and Disorder Act 1998. In 2000, the Lord Chancellor asked Lord Justice Auld to conduct yet another review of the criminal process, published in 2001 as the *Review of the Criminal Courts of England and Wales* but known as the Criminal Courts Review. The Bar Council, Liberty, the Law Society and others published responses and the Government responded in a 2002 white paper (a document outlining legislative plans), *Justice for All*. Many of Auld L.J.'s recommendations were accepted and enacted in the **Courts Act 2003** and the Criminal Justice Act 2003.

LEGAL FRAMEWORK

Common Law Safeguards for the Accused

KEY POINT

Remembering that our legal system is very old and the mother of all common law legal systems worldwide, there are some fundamental safeguards which our courts apply and which we exported to our common law daughters and which formed the model for the **European Convention on Human Rights 1950**.

- *The "rule of law"* means that the authorities must demonstrate a legal basis for the exercise of power.
- The *presumption of innocence* means that the *burden of proof* is always on the prosecutor to prove guilt (although the accused has some burdens in an increasing number of crimes).
- The *right of silence* is not ancient but had come to be seen as a right by the end of the twentieth century.
- The right is part of the ancient common law *privilege against self-incrimination*.
- The *quantum (degree) of proof* in common law criminal justice systems is very high: *proof beyond reasonable doubt*. It is much more difficult to prove a criminal case than a civil one, where the degree of proof is merely "on the balance of probabilities".
- *The requirement for a fair trial* was developed by common law judges in the *rules of natural justice*: the accused has a right to know the case against them and the trial tribunal must not be biased or have an interest in the proceedings.

- Furthermore, given the might of the state against the individual accused, there are certain *protective rules*, such as those restricting prosecution evidence, designed to compensate for that inherent imbalance.
- An accused in detention may apply for a writ of *habeas corpus*, asking the court to declare his detention to be unlawful, under the **Habeas Corpus Act 1679**. This is based on an ancient Anglo-Saxon common law writ, older than **Magna Carta 1215**.
- The right to *speedy trial* and the 500 year old *rule against torture* (explored in *A and Others v SS for the Home Dept (No 2)* [2005] UKHL 71) are ancient common law rules, providing the basis of art.3 and art.5 respectively of the **HR Convention**.

The European Convention on Human Rights 1950

KEY POINT

British lawyers drafted the **European Convention on Human Rights 1950** in the aftermath of World War II and thus incorporated these common law safeguards into the **Convention**. It was made enforceable in our courts since 2000, as a consequence of the **Human Rights Act 1998**. Articles 3, 5 and 6 are most pertinent to criminal procedure. Article 6 provides for a right to a fair trial and art.5 a right to liberty and security.

Article 6 (paraphrased)

- Entitles the accused to a fair and public hearing;
- within a reasonable time; and
- by an independent and impartial tribunal established by law
- He is presumed innocent; and
- has the right to be informed, in detail, of the case against him.
- He must have adequate time and facilities to prepare his defence.
- He may defend himself in person;
- or have a choice of free legal assistance if the interests of justice so require.
- He has the right to examine witnesses; and
- to have an interpreter if he cannot understand the language of the court.

Article 5 (paraphrased)

- Prescribes the circumstances in which a person may be arrested and detained.

- He must be informed why and what he is charged with.
- He must be brought before a judge within a reasonable time or released.
- All detained persons have a right to challenge the lawfulness of their detention.

Article 3 prohibits torture and inhumane and degrading treatment.

The Criminal Procedure Rules 2012

KEY POINT

For centuries, there have been calls for criminal procedure and the criminal law to be codified, as they are throughout Europe and in many common law countries such as the US.

Auld L.J. reiterated this in his *Review* so a new Criminal Procedure Rule Committee was created in 2004 and they devised the first ever set of **Criminal Procedure Rules** in 2005, as a step towards codification. Also, instead of practice rules (guidelines not law) being set out in a mish-mash of Directions, there is now one Consolidated Criminal Practice Direction. The **Criminal Justice Act 2003** prescribes that the Committee must aim, through the Rules, to make the criminal justice system *"accessible fair and efficient"* and the Rules must be simple and be simply expressed. The Rules contain an *"overriding objective"* and rules about case *management*, reminiscent of the **Civil Procedure Rules 1998**, described in Chapter 4. The Lord Chief Justice and Lord Chancellor sought to bring about a "culture change" in the criminal courts, with judges and case managers taking control over case progression. They were concerned about the number of trials that were delayed or ineffective because of lack of preparedness of the lawyers or other agencies, or because of lawyers' delaying tactics. **Rule 1.1** prescribes: "the overriding objective of this new code is that criminal cases be dealt with justly". This includes (paraphrased):

- acquitting the innocent and convicting the guilty;
- dealing with prosecution and defence fairly;
- recognising the defendant's rights;
- respecting the interests of witnesses, victims and jurors; and
- dealing with cases efficiently and speedily.

The case should be dealt with in ways that take into account the gravity of the offence, the complexity of the issues, the severity of the consequences and the needs of other cases. Part 3 places the criminal courts under a *duty to manage* cases actively which was novel in the English criminal courts. This includes:

- early identification of issues and the needs of witnesses;
- timetabling and monitoring case progress;
- ensuring evidence is presented in the shortest and clearest way;
- discouraging delay and unnecessary hearings;
- encouraging co-operation; and
- making use of IT.

Case progression officers are meant to monitor progress pre-trial, by keeping in touch with all parties: prosecution, defence, etc. A judge, magistrate or clerk may manage a case. The court may set out the consequences of failing to comply with directions. This includes penalising lawyers or others, though current research by Darbyshire confirms previous judicial comment that financial penalties are ineffective and inappropriate and are thus seldom used. At some courts, a culture change is still needed. See Denyer at [2008] Crim. L.R. 784. An Effective Trial Management Programme was piloted from 2003. Ineffective trials were reduced from 23 per cent in 2002 to 12 per cent in 2007. Courts can penalise in costs any third party who causes a case to collapse, such as a newspaper publishing a prejudicial pre-trial report.

THE PRE-TRIAL CRIMINAL PROCESS

Prosecutors

The Attorney General (Att Gen)

This is a government minister and their chief legal adviser, responsible for the Treasury Solicitor's Department, CPS, Revenue and Customs Prosecution Office, and Serious Fraud Office. In 2009, the Att Gen published a Protocol setting out her relationship with them. The Att Gen heads the Law Officers' Department and is in overall charge of the prosecution process. The Att Gen's consent is required by statute for prosecutions of national interest or sensitivity (e.g. certain prosecutions under the **Official Secrets Act**). The Att Gen can also enter a *nolle prosequi*, to stop a prosecution (e.g. if it is vexatious or he discovers the defendant is dying).

The Director of Public Prosecutions (DPP)

In addition to heading the CPS and the Serious Organised Crime Agency, dozens of statutes require his consent to prosecution, mostly to serious offences, but he is very seldom involved personally in a decision. In 1997, the Law Commission suggested drastic reduction in the number of offences where the Att Gen's or DPP's consent is required and Auld L.J. agreed, in his 2001 Review. The HL held, in *Kebilene* [2000] 2 A.C. 326 that the DPP's decision to prosecute is not judicially reviewable in the absence of bad faith or dishonesty. In *R (on the application of Purdy) v DPP* [2009] UKHL 45 the law lords ruled that the DPP was obliged to publish his policy identifying the facts and circumstances he would take into account in deciding whether to prosecute someone for assisting the suicide of a terminally ill person.

Public bodies

Many government departments and agencies have statutory prosecution powers.

Private persons

Private prosecutions were preserved on the recommendation of the Royal Commission on Criminal Procedure (RCCP) 1981.

The Crown Prosecution Service (CPS)

This was created as a national prosecution service by the Prosecution of Offences Act 1985, on the recommendation of the RCCP, to allow for a co-ordinated national prosecution policy. The CPS has the discretion to prosecute and stop proceedings. It can ask the police to investigate offences but it cannot order them to do so. It has no investigatory facilities. The Royal Commission on Criminal Justice (RCCJ) 1993 considered whether the CPS should have the power to supervise police investigations, as in Scotland or European jurisdictions. It decided against it. The Narey Report 1997 recommended putting CPS staff into police stations to create a closer working relationship. This was done, despite the criticism that it jeopardises the independence of the CPS.

It also recommended that CPS non-lawyers should be able to prosecute guilty pleas in the magistrates' court and this was permitted by the **Crime and Disorder Act 1998**. This was extended to summary trials (following 'not guilty' pleas) and contested bail applications, by the Criminal Justice and Immigration Act 2008. This was a money-saving exercise, heavily condemned by the Law Society and the Bar Council. An internal CPS survey found that only half the 400 paralegals felt they had enough training. By 2012, many Crown Court cases are prosecuted by CPS employed lawyers, rather than independent barristers as they used to be. This has provoked some judicial criticism of prosecution quality. Since its creation, the CPS has been bedevilled by reports of poor performance, often caused by lack of funding. A 2010 Inspectorate report said poor preparation by the London CPS allowed many defendants to go free.

Prosecution Procedure: Charging and Prosecuting

The Criminal Justice Act 2003 Sch.2 provides that the custody police officer must refer to guidance from the DPP. This indicates which cases should be referred to the CPS and lists those defendants who should be bailed. The Act (s.29) introduced a new way of initiating criminal proceedings. A written charge may be issued by the police or a prosecutor, with a requisition to appear in court. Allowing prosecutors to issue charges was introduced because they, being lawyers, were more likely to select the appropriate charges than police officers. This was introduced in 2004, after pilot schemes resulted in a 40 per cent increase in early guilty pleas and a 90 per cent decrease in discontinued, ineffective or changed cases. The CPS is guided in its decisions whether to prosecute by the *Code for Crown Prosecutors*. It applies a two-stage test on *evidential sufficiency* and *public interest*. (See CPS website. The code is in plain language and continually updated, after public consultation). The DPP has published many sets of more detailed prosecution criteria on specific offences, from assisting suicide to football related offences. There is no obligation to prosecute all crimes, in contrast with some European jurisdictions. A decision not to prosecute is not normally judicially reviewable but see the following section.

Cautions, Fixed Penalty Notices and Deferred Prosecution Agreements

Police detainees may be released with no further action or officially cautioned, including conditionally cautioned, if they admit an offence. Most young offenders are cautioned. The 2003 Act permits the CPS to issue a conditional caution, where there is sufficient evidence to charge a suspect with an offence which he or she admits, and the suspect agrees. If the suspect fails to comply with the conditions he may be prosecuted for the offence. The formal caution was recommended by Auld L.J. to replace the informal and piecemeal schemes which were developed casually by the police over the twentieth century. Cautioning for young offenders was put on a statutory footing in the **Crime and Disorder Act 1998**. The Labour government's next tactic to save money was to allow the police to issue fixed penalty notices on the street for public order offences, thus reducing the number of people processed by the magistrates' court. In 2009, the Government launched a review of these out-of-court disposals, prompted by public concern, including a *Panorama* programme about people committing violent assaults and being cautioned instead of prosecuted. This included the story of Mr Guest, seriously injured by a burglar. The "astonishing" decision not to prosecute was quashed by the High Court in judicial review: *R. (on the application of Guest) v DPP* [2009] EWHC 594. In a 2010 speech, Leveson L.J. questioned the use of over 450,000 FPNs and cautions per year. In 2011, HM Inspectorate of Constabulary and HMCPS Inspectorate published a joint condemnatory report of out-of-court disposals. The **Legal Aid, Sentencing and Punishment of Offenders Act 2012** allows chief constables to set up schemes allowing police officers to attach educational requirements to the FPNs they impose, so that offenders can be required to pay for and attend courses about the social or health consequences of their offending. PNs for disorder cannot be imposed on children.

In 2012, the Coalition Government announced they might offer "deferred prosecution agreements" to companies instead of prosecuting them. They would have to admit wrongdoing, pay a penalty and obey certain conditions. This will not satisfy critics who already think white collar criminals get off lightly.

The previous Labour government was interested in promoting community justice and neighbourhood courts, and the Coalition Government is extending this. In their 2012 white paper, *Swift and Sure Justice*, they said

> "Neighbourhood Justice Panels are a partnership between local agencies, police and local authorities, and the local community. They seek to address anti-social behaviour and low level offending where this can appropriately be dealt with in and by the community, through a restorative solution focused on addressing the needs of the victim, repairing the harm done to the community, and avoiding unnecessary criminalisation (particularly of young people)."

This provides a practical solution to "net-widening", a concern in the 1980s and 1990s that children were being put through court and labelled as offenders for behaviour that would have been classed as naughtiness in the early-twentieth century, and perhaps resulted in a telling-off by the local police.

Bail

Most people are tried in magistrates' courts and are not remanded at all, in custody or on bail. The police may grant bail at the police station and the **Criminal Justice Act 2003** enables "street bail" from the scene of the arrest (s.4). The Bail Act 1976 introduced a statutory right to bail. Magistrates could refuse bail only if they believe the defendant will fail to surrender to custody, or commit an offence or interfere with witnesses. The court must have regard to the nature and seriousness of the offence, the probable disposal of the defendant, his character and community ties, etc., his previous bail record and the strength of evidence against him.

During the late 1980s, concern arose over the number of offences committed whilst on bail. The Criminal Justice and Public Order Act 1994 added another exception to the right to bail, where the defendant was already on bail at the time of the alleged new offence. This was amended in the **Criminal Justice Act 2003**. There is now a *presumption* that bail will not be granted in these circumstances to an adult unless the court is satisfied that there is no significant risk of his re-offending whilst on bail (s.13). There is also a *presumption* that an adult who has failed to surrender to custody will not be granted bail, unless the court is satisfied that there is no significant risk that he would so fail if released (s.15). There is a *presumption* against bail for certain Class A drug users (s.19). The 1994 Act prohibited bail for those charged with murder, rape, manslaughter and attempts of those crimes, where they had previously been convicted of such an offence. Because of the **European Convention on HR**, this had to be amended by the **Crime and Disorder Act 1998**, to permit the court to grant bail in exceptional circumstances, because under the **Convention**, a state cannot make a blanket ban on bail for a group of offenders. Bail may be granted by the police, or magistrates' court or Crown Court. A magistrates' clerk (legal adviser) may renew bail and any court must consider bail at each court appearance. Both prosecution and defence may appeal a bail decision. The **Legal Aid, Sentencing and Punishment of Offenders Act 2012** introduces restrictions on the courts' powers to remand adults and children in custody where there is no real prospect that they would be sentenced to custody if convicted. This is a new cost-saving measure because the Government is concerned to cut down the number of prisoners.

The right of silence and the privilege against self-incrimination

The right is a common law right (not ancient) and is closely related to the privilege, again a common law concept, now recognised as part of art.6 of the **Convention**. The right of silence exists at three stages: on the street; under interrogation; and at trial. Until the **Criminal Justice and Public Order Act 1994**, the defendant had an unfettered right to silence and the judge could comment to the jury if a defendant remained silent but could not comment adversely. The right was considered by the Criminal Law Revision Committee 1972, the RCCP 1981 and the RCCJ 1993 and it has long been a subject of controversy.

Proponents hail it as a major (almost symbolic) safeguard of the English legal system that the defendant cannot convict himself out of his own mouth. It leaves the burden of proof entirely on the prosecution.

Opponents say it is a rule protecting the guilty; it encourages the police to intimidate suspects into confessing and it is sentimental to argue that the accused should not be allowed to convict himself.

From 1987, Conservative Home Secretaries contemplated limiting the right, because they thought professional criminals took advantage of it. Pre-1994, one major inroad which provoked criticism was the power of the Serious Fraud Office (SFO) to require answers to written questions. In *Saunders v UK* (1997) 23 E.H.R.R. 313 the European Court of Human Rights (ECtHR) ruled that statutory powers to require a defendant to answer questions pre-trial offended against the privilege against self-incrimination so the offending legislation and similar Acts were amended by the UK Parliament to prevent answers gained being used in evidence. The Court has ruled that the requirement that the defendant submit to blood and urine tests does not breach the privilege. They also ruled that there is no violation of the privilege by asking car owners to disclose driver details when caught on a speed camera: *Francis v UK* (25624/02) (2008) 46 E.H.R.R. 21.

The RCCJ 1993 considered the issue and recommended that the right of silence under interrogation should be retained and that only after the prosecution case had been fully disclosed should the defendant be required to answer charges, or risk an adverse comment at trial on any new, undisclosed defence (an "ambush defence"). The **1994 Act** went much further than this and, critics said, abrogated the right to silence and, as can be seen below, caused a lot of confusion and appeals. Sections 34–39 allow the court to draw "such inferences as appear proper" from the accused's failure to mention, under police questioning, any fact which he could have been expected to mention, or failure to account for any objects, marks or substances, or to account for his presence at a particular place, or to give evidence or answer questions at trial. In *Murray v UK* (1996) 22 E.H.R.R. 29 the ECtHR considered legal advice crucial to a defendant who exercised his right of silence. In *Condron v UK* (2001) 31 E.H.R.R. 1, the ECtHR held, applying art.6, that it was inappropriate to draw an adverse inference, under the **1994 Act**, where defendants had maintained silence on their lawyer's advice. In *R. v Beckles* [2004] EWCA Crim 2766, the CA held that where a solicitor's advice was relied on, the jury should decide whether the facts relied on at trial were facts which the defendant could reasonably have been expected to mention at interview. If not, that is the end of the matter. Under the revised direction, the jury is asked to consider whether the defendant genuinely and reasonably relied on legal advice to remain silent. See now *R. v Bresa* [2005] EWCA Crim 1414 and *R. v Hoare and Pierce* [2005] EWCA Crim 784. Judges must weigh the public interest in having D's account against his wellbeing: *R v Tabbakh* [2009] EWCA Crim 464.

Mode of Trial—Crown Court or Magistrates' Court?

KEY POINT

Indictable cases have to be tried in the Crown Court and summary offences in the magistrates' court but in the category of median seriousness, "triable either way", called "either way" cases, the magistrates may send a case up to the Crown Court, if they consider it too serious. If they have no preference, the defendant may elect to be dealt with by the Crown Court.

The RCCJ 1993 considered that many (expensive) Crown Court cases could more appropriately be dealt with in the (much cheaper) magistrates' court. (In 2012, the present Government is still concerned). It recommended removing the defendant's right to elect trial in the Crown Court and thus jury trial. While research had shown that the acquittal rate was higher in the Crown Court, in matched cases, sentencing was harsher. The Home Office published a 1995 consultation paper on *Mode of Trial*, suggesting three options for resolving the problem that trivial cases were sent up to the (expensive) Crown Court and nevertheless given sentences within the magistrates' powers:

- classifying more offences as summary only;
- removing the defendant's right to elect; or
- requiring magistrates to ask defendants to indicate their plea before taking a decision on mode of trial.

The Government enacted the third option, in s.49 of the Criminal Procedure and Investigations Act 1996, known as the *plea before venue* procedure (now extended by the **Criminal Justice Act 2003**). The intention is that *magistrates will hear all either-way cases where the defendant indicates a guilty plea*, unless the magistrates consider their sentencing powers too low. Even before the section was brought into force, the 1997 Narey Report again suggested dispensing with the defendant's right to elect. In 1998, the Home Secretary published a consultation, *Determining Mode of Trial in Either Way Cases*. He set out the familiar arguments, as follows.

For abolition of the defendant's right to elect (Crown Court jury trial)

- The right only dated from 1855 and had nothing to do with **Magna Carta 1215**.
- Thousands of defendants chose Crown Court trial but most changed their plea to guilty after significant inconvenience and worry to witnesses, and considerable cost.
- By definition, defence-elected cases are those which magistrates have determined are suitable for them. The mode of trial decision should be based on objective assessment by the court of the gravity of the case, not the defendant's perception of what is advantageous to him.
- It was questionable whether defendants opted for jury trial to defend their reputation: nine-tenths of those opting already had convictions.
- Most defendants elected jury trial because they wanted to delay proceedings, to apply pressure to the Crown to accept a guilty plea to a lesser offence, or to deter witnesses.
- Few other countries allowed the defendant a choice.

Arguments in favour of the right

- The right helped to promote confidence in the criminal justice system.
- Whereas magistrates were concerned with the seriousness of the offence, it was the defendant's reputation which the public saw as justifying the right to elect.
- People usually defended the right because they would want jury trial if they were charged with something of which they were innocent.
- People assumed that Crown Court trial was fairer. Defendants mainly elected because they rightly believed they had a higher chance of acquittal.
- Some arguments went to merits of jury trial, for example, the jury's capacity to acquit contrary to legal proof of guilt, applying jury "equity", as discussed in the jury chapter.

The Home Secretary introduced the Criminal Justice (Mode of Trial) Bill in 1999, to abolish the right and leave the decision to magistrates. It was condemned by the Bar, the Law Society, the Society of Black Lawyers and civil rights groups such as the Legal Action Group (LAG), who argued the following:

- Defendants usually opted for jury trial because they rightly saw their chances of obtaining justice in the Crown Court as significantly higher. In 1997, 62 per cent of defendants who pleaded not guilty to some or all counts were acquitted. Having a professional judge oversee the case was as important as having a jury. 54 per cent were acquitted because the judge discharged the case or directed an acquittal.
- Electing jury trial triggered other safeguards, such as greater prosecution disclosure.
- Removing the right would disadvantage black defendants. They more frequently chose the Crown Court.
- Other procedural changes would minimise defendants' manipulation of the system.

Wolchover and Heaton-Armstrong at (1998) 148 N.L.J. 1614, added that loss of liberty was no less serious for an habitual thief than loss of good name for someone with no previous convictions. Courtney Griffiths QC (*Counsel*, April 1999) added these points:

- Research by the Runnymede Trust, 1990, showed that, whereas under one third of white defendants elected for jury trial, 45 per cent of black defendants did.
- This was an intelligent choice. Only two per cent of magistrates were (*then*) non-white. Research showed white defendants had a substantially better chance of being bailed and were less likely to receive immediate custodial sentences.

A number of commentators emphasised that jury trial was inherently superior to summary trial.

- Listing for Crown Court trial triggered a much more careful review of the evidence by the CPS, which often resulted in their dropping the case or reducing the charges. This implied that if magistrates were to decide on mode of trial they would be doing so on inadequate information.
- At the Crown Court, a professional judge reviewed the strength and admissibility of the evidence, whereas magistrates were both fact-finders and arbiters of the law.

Some critics pointed out that:

- magistrates' courts were seen as police courts; and/or
- magistrates were considered part of the Establishment and they were not as socially and ethnically diverse as the jury.

The first Bill was heavily defeated in the House of Lords in 2000. The Home Secretary replaced it with another, which was again defeated in 2000. Auld L.J., in the Criminal Courts Review 2001, again recommended removing the right to elect. This again attracted ferocious opposition from the legal profession and others, repeating the arguments above, so by the time it wrote its 2002 White Paper *Justice for All*, the Government had abandoned the idea and instead announced that it would increase magistrates' sentencing powers (thus by other means achieving their aim of shifting more work down to the magistrates' court).

With the same aim, the Government also introduced provisions in the **Criminal Justice Act 2003** to change the mode of trial decision-making procedure yet again, with a view to making the decisions of both magistrates and defendant better informed. These followed the recommendations in the Criminal Courts Review. The Act provides that, before deciding on mode of trial, the magistrates should be told of the defendant's previous convictions. They must give prosecution and defence a chance to air their views and take account of allocation guidelines issued by the *Sentencing Council*. If the court decides the case is suitable for summary trial, it must explain so to the defendant, in ordinary language, and tell him he can choose a Crown Court trial but that, if the charge is of a certain violent or sexual offence, it can still commit him there for sentence if, having tried the case, it thinks its sentencing powers are too low. The defendant can then request an indication of the sentence he might get if he were to plead guilty in the magistrates' court but the court is not obliged to provide this. If it does, it must allow the defendant an opportunity to reconsider his plea. If it decides to send him to the Crown Court, or he elects a Crown Court trial, it must transfer him direct, under s.51 of the **Crime and Disorder Act 1998**, without a committal. The Coalition Government, from 2010, is again concerned that too many trivial cases are going up to the Crown Court so in their 2012 white paper, *Swift and Sure Justice*, they say they will introduce legislation to stop magistrates sending overly trivial theft and handling cases up to the Crown Court, while retaining the defendant's right to elect. This is quite ingenious because it avoids the public outcry the would be provoked by eroding the defendant's right to choose.

Committal proceedings

Almost all defendants in the Crown Court used to be committed for trial by magistrates, whose job it was to certify that there was a *prima facie* case against them. Mostly, this was a swift, paper exercise. It was abolished for indictable offences by s.51 of the **Crime and Disorder Act 1998**. The magistrates may transfer defendants directly to the Crown Court and, as explained, this has been extended to either-way offences by the **Criminal Justice Act 2003** BUT it is only just being brought into force, experimentally, in 2012.

Pre-trial disclosure of evidence

Requirements for pre-trial disclosure had become more demanding since 1981, when the Att Gen had generally required the prosecution to make available to the defence all unused material. The picture became more complex after miscarriages of justice were exposed in the early 1990s. Courts found it difficult to balance the defendant's interest in seeing all the evidence gathered and the prosecution's interest in keeping sensitive material (such as the identity of an informant). The RCCJ 1993 recommended a statutory scheme of disclosure. It was anxious to stop "ambush defences", where an unpredictable defence is raised at trial. This was effected by ss.34–39 of the **Criminal Justice and Public Order Act 1994**, which qualify the defendant's right of silence (see below).

The **Criminal Procedure and Investigations Act 1996** Pt I, enacted a statutory scheme of disclosure for Crown Court cases. The prosecutor had a two-stage duty to disclose to the defence all unused material that might, in his opinion, undermine the prosecution case. The accused could give a written defence statement, in order to obtain secondary disclosure. If he did not do so he risked the judge inviting the jury to draw a negative inference from his failure. The **1996 Act** was criticised as allowing the prosecutor to choose what to disclose and for punishing the accused for not making a defence statement, thus eroding the principle of innocence until guilt is proven. In practice, defence statements were criticised as being so vague they were useless. (They were usually a couple of sentences.)

Auld L.J. examined these criticisms. Consequently, the Government amended the **1996 Act** in the **Criminal Justice Act 2003**. The Act replaced the old two-stage test with a single objective test, requiring the prosecutor to disclose material that has not previously been disclosed and which might reasonably be considered capable of undermining the case for the prosecution against the accused, or of assisting the case for the accused. It replaces the secondary disclosure stage with a revised continuing duty on the prosecutor to disclose material that meets the new test. The prosecutor is specifically required to review the prosecution material on receipt of the defence statement and to make further disclosure if required under the continuing duty.

It also amends defence disclosure requirements. The accused must provide a more detailed defence statement, setting out any particular defences on which he intends to rely and indicating any points of law he wishes to take, including any points as to the admissibility of evidence or abuse of process. The judge must warn the accused about any failure to comply with the defence statement requirements, because the judge may still invite the jury to draw an adverse inference if the defence statement is inadequate. But there is no other sanction against a recalcitrant defendant: see case law analysed in *R. v Malcolm* [2011] EWCA Crim 2069 and comment at [2012] Crim. L.R. 238. An updated defence statement may be required to assist the management of the trial, requiring the accused to serve details of his witnesses and experts. In 2006, the CA issued *A Protocol for the Control and Management of Unused Material for the Crown Court*. It called for a "culture change". It was the *prosecutor's* duty to inspect everything. Judges should inspect the defence statement to ensure that it complied with the statutory requirement. In 2011, the Ministry of Justice conducted yet another review of disclosure.

The Plea

In common law countries, once the accused has pleaded guilty, the prosecutor does not need to prove the case, by bringing evidence and examining witnesses. There is no trial. Once the court accepts a guilty plea, the defendant is "proved guilty according to law", under art.6 (2): *Revitt v DPP* [2006] EWHC 2266 (Admin). In England and Wales, as in most common law jurisdictions, well over 90 per cent of defendants plead guilty. Following a guilty plea, there is a brief court appearance in either the magistrates' court or the Crown Court, depending on seriousness. The prosecution present a brief version of their case, "the facts", as they always call it; the accused may then make a plea in mitigation of sentence, asking for certain factors to be taken into account to lessen his sentence, then the magistrates or judge will sentence him. They may adjourn sentencing to require a pre-sentence or psychiatric report on the offender.

Plea bargaining and sentence discounts

This means that the accused agrees to plead guilty in exchange for:

- an offer of a lower sentence;
- a reduction in charge to a less serious offence (charge bargaining); or
- a promise by the prosecution to present a less serious version of the facts (fact bargaining).

The first, well-known and widely used in the US, was generally impracticable here because judges could not take part in it, under the old rules laid down in *Turner* [1970] 2 Q.B. 321 and because prosecutors cannot generally recommend sentences, unlike American prosecutors, who routinely do deals over plea and sentence with the defence. *R. v Turner*, affirmed by a 1976 Practice Direction, held that counsel could advise the defendant (how to plead) in strong terms, provided he made it clear that the defendant had a free choice. Generally, the judge should "never indicate the sentence which he is minded to impose" and never indicate he would impose a severer sentence following a not guilty plea. He could not indicate that, having read the papers, he would impose a certain type of sentence, following a guilty plea. A judge *was* permitted to say that, whatever the plea, the sentence would take a particular form.

Nevertheless, there was persistent concern about the resources wasted by defendants pleading not guilty then changing their plea at the last minute, after an expensive Crown Court trial had been prepared (called a "cracked trial"). Some judges rewarded defendants with a sentence discount of up to one third in exchange for an early guilty plea, but practice was diverse and, historically, magistrates did not give sentencing discounts. Successive governments were concerned, in the 1990s, to stop the waste caused by cracked trials. The RCCJ 1993 recommended that the system of rewarding defendants for pleading guilty should be formalised. The earlier the guilty plea, the higher the sentence discount. Judges should be permitted to indicate, in advance of trial, the highest sentence they were prepared to give. Only the first part of the recommendation was enacted, in s.48 of the **Criminal Justice and Public Order Act 1994** (now repeated in the **Criminal Justice Act 2003** ss.144 and 174). This puts a duty on the court, in sentencing a guilty pleader, to take into account the stage at which he pleaded guilty, and to announce in open court any resultant sentence reduction. This simply formalised the existing practice of rewards for early guilty pleas.

In his 2001 Criminal Courts Review, Auld L.J. reiterated the RCCJ's 1993 call for a formalised system of graduated sentencing discounts for guilty pleas, coupled with a system of advanced indication of sentence. The Government responded that it intended to introduce a clearer tariff of sentence discounts. This is not incorporated in the **Criminal Justice Act 2003** but was announced by Lord Chancellor Falconer in 2003, as part of the Case Preparation Project (see below). In 2011–12, the criminal courts are experimenting with an Early Guilty Plea project, offering a more explicit system of discounts for guilty pleas, with the maximum discount and speedy processing to those who plead guilty at the first opportunity, in the magistrates' court. The latest plans for speedy justice are contained in the July 2012 white paper, *Swift and Sure Justice* but they follow hard on the heels of a similar scheme by New Labour.

KEY POINT

The **Sentencing Council** published guidelines (on its website) on a graduated structure of sentence discounts for guilty pleas to be applied in the Crown Court from 2005. A maximum one-third discount should be given to those who plead guilty at the earliest opportunity in the police station. Those found guilty after a not guilty plea and trial get no discount. The sliding scale applied even if the defendant was caught red-handed. In ***R. v Goodyear (Practice Note)*** [2005] EWCA Crim 888, a five-judge CA laid down what judges should do in this "different culture". They re-emphasised that the defendant's plea must be made voluntarily and free from improper pressure but this did not preclude the defendant from seeking an **advance indication of sentence**. They laid down guidelines:

- The judge should confine himself to indicating the maximum sentence for a guilty plea at that point.
- He could only act at the request of the defendant, not on his own initiative, or that of the defence lawyer.
- He could refuse a sentence indication but, once given, it was binding on him and other judges.
- A hypothetical indication should be refused.
- A judge should not be invited to give an indication on the basis of a plea bargain.
- He should not be asked to indicate levels of sentence dependent on different pleas.
- The defence advocate was responsible for ensuring that his client appreciated that he should not plead guilty unless he was guilty and that any sentence indication remained subject to the Att Gen's right to appeal against an unduly lenient sentence.

Although these guidelines warn judges not to participate in plea bargaining, the system of rewarding people for guilty pleas by offering sentence discounts inevitably results in bargaining between prosecution and defence. Some find this practice offensive and dangerous, not least because some innocent people are persuaded to plead guilty and because those who exercise their right to trial are punished with a sentence 50 per cent heavier than those who confess at the police station, and thirdly because giving people a sentence discount when they are caught red-handed destroys the system of just deserts. This problem led to public outcry in 2006 when judges were targeted by the *Sun* newspaper for passing lenient sentences on violent offenders and paedophiles (and announcing that the offender's sentence would normally be cut by parole, early release and so on). The Home Secretary, John Reid, joined in the criticism until it was pointed out to him that his own department devised the parole rules and that judges had felt obliged to follow the Sentencing (Guidelines) Council's discount scheme. One case was referred to the Court of Appeal (Criminal Division) (CACD) by the Att Gen. The CACD said that the trial judge had been correct in applying the one-third discount: *Attorney General's Refs Nos 14 and 15 of 2006 (Tanya French and Alan Robert Webster)* [2006] EWCA Crim 1335. The SGC urgently reviewed the Guidelines, following consultation, especially in relation to cases like this, where people are caught red-handed and the prosecution case is so overwhelming that they have no grounds for pleading not guilty. In such cases, only a 20 per cent discount need be given. (See discussion in *R v Wilson*, at [2012] Crim. L.R. 560). In 2011 the Justice Minister caused public outcry by repeating a proposal to offer 50 per cent sentence discounts for guilty pleaders.

The **Serious Organised Crime and Police Act 2005** ss.71–75, introduced a type of statutory, formalised plea bargaining. The Serious Organised Crime Agency (SOCA) can offer an offender contractual immunity from prosecution and a reduction in sentence in exchange for assistance in investigation and prosecution. The CA gave guidelines in *R. v P* [2007] EWCA Crim 2290. Additionally, it has been common practice in any type of serious case to offer immunity or sentence discounts to suspects who are prepared to give prosecution evidence. The courts have upheld these bargains by giving astonishingly big discounts of up to two thirds off a sentence. This contractual bargaining is sinister to those of us who are concerned that we are importing American-style plea bargaining. The Att Gen, exasperated with the collapse of so many expensive fraud trials, such as the Jubilee Line trial discussed in the jury chapter, planned ways of persuading more people to plead guilty, rather than risking expensive jury trials where the jury might well acquit or the trial collapse. Following the government's 2006 *Fraud Review*, the Att Gen consulted in 2008 on offering binding pre-trial bargains, as above. (See now the Att Gen's guidelines on plea discussions in fraud cases.) Lake warns that it seems to have been forgotten that we have already tried offering witness immunity from prosecution, in the Northern Irish "supergrass" system, to obtain evidence against terrorists. Hundreds of convictions were overturned because the system was perceived to be open to abuse. Obviously, the convicted individual could argue that the witness was unreliable, since they were bribed to give evidence with a promise of freedom: (2006) 156 N.L.J. 908. De Grazia and Hyland advocated greater use of prosecutors' deals with defendants, in exchange for assistance: [2011] Crim. L.R. 357. In *R. v Innospec* [2010] Crim. L.R. 665, though, Thomas L.J. reminded us that in England and

Wales, the prosecutor had no legal power to enter into an agreement as to penalty.

Trial by judge alone

In the magistrates' court, a defendant may be dealt with by a bench of lay magistrates or a district judge (magistrates' court) sitting alone. He has no choice. In the Crown Court, following recommendations by Auld L.J., the **Criminal Justice Act 2003** s.44 allows the judge to direct a judge-only trial where he is satisfied that there is a "real and present danger that jury tampering would take place". See jury chapter.

KEY POINT

The Act would have permitted the prosecution to apply for a judge-only trial in long or complex fraud trials **but the Government never implemented this**, promising to reconsider, as it was bitterly opposed in and out of Parliament. Following the collapse of the expensive Jubilee Line fraud trial, the Government attempted to reintroduce this measure, in the **Fraud (Trials without a Jury) Bill 2006–07** but it was defeated. This is explained further in the jury chapter.

In 2002, the Law Commission suggested a two-stage procedure to prosecute multiple offences and this resulted in s.13 of the **Domestic Violence, Crime and Victims Act 2004**. If the jury convicts on a sample count, the other counts may be tried by judge alone. Some critics accused the government of sneaking in non-jury trials in a fairly obscure Act.

Case management hearings in the Crown Court

Since 1995 a plea and directions hearing, now called a plea and case management hearing (**Criminal Procedure Rules** Pt 15), may be arranged prior to trial. This is very brief, designed to prepare for the trial and fix a trial date. In all class 1 or serious or complex cases, the prosecution provides a summary, identifying issues of law and fact and estimating trial length. The accused is arraigned and his plea entered. Following a not guilty plea, the parties are expected to inform the court of witnesses and any special requirements for trial. If the plea is guilty, the judge should, if possible, proceed to sentence after hearing a plea in mitigation. Where the judge is considering a custodial sentence or non-custodial alternative he may require a pre-sentence report or, where appropriate, a psychiatric or medical report. The **Criminal Procedure Rules** leave it to the Case Progression Officer to monitor trial preparation and communicate with the parties about timetabling. It is up to the lawyers to certify that the case is ready for trial.

Pre-trial hearings in the Crown Court

These are not new but were put onto a statutory footing by the **Criminal Procedure and Investigations Act 1996**. The judge may order a preparatory hearing for one of the following purposes: identifying important issues; assisting the jury's comprehension; expediting proceedings; or assisting the judge's trial management. She may hear arguments and rule on points of law and admissibility of evidence. She may require detailed case statements and require the prosecution evidence and any explanatory material to be prepared in a form which she considers is likely to help the jury understand it.

Speeding up justice

Most recommendations of the 1997 Narey Report were enacted in the **Crime and Disorder Act 1998**. The magistrates' courts where the reforms were piloted cut the disposal time of all offenders by around two-thirds. Here are the main points.

- CPS staff were placed in police stations to advise on charges; non-lawyers were permitted to prosecute in the magistrates' court, as mentioned above.
- Early first hearings for straightforward guilty pleas were introduced in magistrates' courts.
- Early administrative hearings were introduced in contested cases.
- Case management powers were given to clerks and single magistrates.
- A Youth Justice Board, Youth Offending Teams and a set of new procedures were created, to speed up and co-ordinate the processing, treatment and rehabilitation of young offenders. The Coalition Government threatened to abolish the YJB but by 2012, it still exists.

In its 2002 White Paper, *Justice for All*, the Labour Government expressed the aim to make trials faster. From 2003, it published performance tables for the 42 criminal justice areas which then existed. Lord Falconer L.C. announced the Case Preparation Project, with Case Progression Officers, and this eventually resulted in the case management procedure prescribed by the **Criminal Procedure Rules**, above. Very controversially, lawyers have been given financial incentives for early and proper preparation of cases, and defendants, as we have seen, are rewarded with graduated sentence discounts for earlier guilty pleas. Defendants who fail to attend lawyers' appointments may be imprisoned for breach of bail conditions.

The government introduced a *simple, speedy summary justice system* for magistrates' courts, from about 2003, but researchers questioned its claims of success. In 2006, the House of Commons Public Accounts Committee said that, in 2004–5, just under two thirds of magistrates' court trials and over a quarter of pre-trial hearings did not proceed, wasting £173 million of taxpayers' money. From 2008, they introduced virtual hearings from the police station, where the offender "appears" in the magistrates' court via a TV link from the police station and is dealt with by magistrates immediately.

THE CRIMINAL *AND CIVIL* TRIAL PROCESS

Trials occur in a tiny fraction of cases. Over 90 per cent of defendants to criminal charges plead guilty and thus appear in court only to offer a plea in mitigation and to be sentenced. In the civil courts, most cases are settled by negotiation between the parties, or judgment is entered in default, because the defendant has not entered a defence. There are significant differences between civil and criminal trials, such as the degree of proof required, and evidential differences, such as the rule against hearsay. The adversarial model cannot apply as well to criminal trials as it does to civil because the defendant is faced with such a powerful opponent, the state.

The judge as arbiter

Essentially, the judge acts as an unbiased umpire whose job it is to listen to evidence presented by both sides, without interfering in the preparation of the case, or the presentation of evidence or arguments (legal or factual) at trial. This is often contrasted with the role of European investigating magistrates, or the Scottish procurator fiscal who may direct criminal investigations, cross-examine the defendant and collect evidence for the trial court. There is no English equivalent. The judge does not normally summon witnesses and must generally leave the examination of witnesses, in court, to the parties. In *Jones v National Coal Board* [1957] 2 Q.B. 55 Lord Denning M.R. summarised the judge's role in the trial hearing. The judge should;

- listen to all the evidence, only interfering to clarify neglected or obscure points;
- see that advocates behave and stick to the rules;
- exclude irrelevancies and discourage repetition;
- make sure he or she understands the advocates' points; and
- at the end, make up his mind where the truth lies. (In a criminal trial and civil trials, this is the job of the jury, or magistrates in the magistrates' court.)

If a judge interferes unduly in the conduct of a trial, the decision may be quashed because of a breach of the rules of natural justice (fair trial). Though judges leave it to the parties to present evidence, specialist judges, such as those of the Commercial or Admiralty Court, are appointed because of their expertise and are expected to use it. If an advocate forgets a vital precedent in legal argument, the judge can invite argument on it. The rule of non-intervention does not apply in some instances, as follows.

- Where legal argument is addressed to the judge: judges are often in a dialogue with lawyers, especially in the appeal courts.
- In small claims in the county court most parties are unrepresented and need considerable help from the judge. The **Civil Procedure Rules 1998** permit the judge to choose appropriate procedure.
- Where a defendant is unrepresented, mostly in the magistrates' courts and in frequently in all civil courts, he is dependent on the good will and expertise of the Bench and clerk to help him put his case and examine witnesses and explain what is being asked of him.

The role of the magistrates' clerk (legal adviser)

In magistrates' court trials, the clerk has an important role set down in case law, statute and Practice Directions. Magistrates are wholly dependent on their clerks for advice on law, practice, procedure and sentencing. The court clerk, by far the most prevalent legal adviser to magistrates, enjoyed no legal recognition whatever in this role until the enactment of s.117 of the **Courts and Legal Services Act 1990**. The main clerk is the justices' clerk. Their advisory role is set out in the **Courts Act 2003** s.28. It "declares" his functions to include giving advice to justices, on request, about law, practice and procedure, and empowers him to draw their attention to these matters at any time. See also the **Consolidated Criminal Practice Direction** and the **Justices' Clerks Rules 2005**.

The adversarial method of eliciting testimony

The parties are kept to a fixed order of speeches, in the question and answer method.

1. Prosecution (criminal trial) or claimant (civil trial) makes his opening speech.
2. His first witness is examined by him or his legal representative. In civil cases, under the **Civil Procedure Rules 1998**, a pre-trial witness statement normally serves as his evidence-in-chief. Undisputed testimony in civil and criminal cases may be admitted as a statement.
3. This witness is then cross-examined by the opposition.
4. Each witness is so examined until the end of the prosecution/claimant's case.
5. At this point, the defence may invite the judge to decide that there is

"no case to answer", because insufficient evidence has been brought to prove the case. It is up to the person bringing the case to prove it, not up to the defence to disprove it, generally speaking. In criminal trials, the **Criminal Justice Act 2003** Pt 9 introduced a facility for the prosecution to appeal against a judge's ruling of no case to answer or any other evidentiary ruling in which the judge has terminated the trial.

6. The defendant is examined by the defence advocate then cross-examined by the prosecution/claimant. In civil trials, see 2 above.
7. All the defence witnesses are so questioned.
8. The defence sum up.
9. The claimant/prosecution may reply.
10. In a Crown Court jury trial, the judge sums up the evidence for the jury and directs them on law.
11. In any jury trial, criminal or civil, the jury deliberate in secret. In a criminal trial, if the jury cannot reach a unanimous verdict (12–0), then the judge may permit a majority verdict (11–1 or 10–2) and failing any agreement, the jury are called a "hung jury" and the case must be dismissed but a retrial may be ordered.
12. In a civil case, if the judge (or, rarely, jury) finds the case proven "on the balance of probabilities", he must find for the claimant and make an order, normally in damages. In a criminal case, if the magistrates', or DJMC, or jury, find guilt proven "beyond reasonable doubt" they must convict the defendant. The defendant may then be sentenced by the magistrates or DJMC in the magistrates' court, or the judge in the Crown Court.
13. If the criminal case is not proven, the defendant is found "not guilty" and acquitted and is discharged. If the civil case is not proven, the judge dismisses it and may order costs against the unsuccessful claimant.

This strict order of proceedings is meant to guarantee "fair play". In criminal trials, each witness stays outside the courtroom until called, so they cannot copy a previous witness, and the witness is strictly kept to answering the questions put. If she tries to add points, or pass an opinion, she is quickly stopped by the judge or advocates. This results in two problems.

- If the witness feels she has vital evidence to add, she has no way of volunteering it. This can be especially frustrating to the expert witness, examined by non-experts. The RCCJ 1993 recommended that where expert evidence is disputed in criminal trials, the judge should invite the expert witness to say whether they wish to add to their evidence.

- This system is dependent on the expertise of the advocate to bring out all and only that relevant information helpful to his case.

Advocates are not allowed to "lead" their witnesses, i.e. ask questions which suggest an answer, unless the judge and opposition consent. The very aim of cross-examination is, however, to *mis*lead.

THE CRIMINAL TRIAL

The defendant is provided with certain safeguards in the criminal trial to restore the balance slightly against the heavy weight of the state. The criminal quantum (standard) of proof is "beyond reasonable doubt", so it is much harder to prove a criminal case than a civil one, where the case must be proven "on the balance of probabilities". The accused has a right of silence though there have been inroads into this since 1994, as above. Certain evidence is excluded because it is unduly prejudicial against the defendant, inherently unreliable, or its utterance is against the public interest. Auld L.J. concluded, in his 2001 Review, however, that we should move away from the strict rule against the admission of certain evidence in criminal proceedings to a more flexible position where we admit such evidence and instead trust fact-finders to assess the weight of the evidence. The Government agreed with him in the White Paper, *Justice for All* (2002). Accordingly, the **Criminal Justice Act 2003** modifies certain of these exclusory rules and we can expect further such modifications to the law of criminal evidence. Below are some examples of evidence which is generally excluded.

1. *Defendant's previous convictions*, with certain exceptions. Following recommendations by the Law Commission and Auld L.J., the **Criminal Justice Act 2003** (in ss.98–113) replaces all common law and statutory provisions with a comprehensive set of rules for the admissibility of previous misconduct evidence.
2. *Communications between client and legal adviser*, without permission.
3. *Hearsay evidence*: the basic rule was that evidence could not be related to the court unless its author was there to present it. It applied to spoken words and documents. It was thought to be unfair to rely on the evidence of a witness who was not present to be cross-examined. The hearsay rule was subject to so many exceptions that it was very difficult to apply. The RCCJ 1993 recommended that hearsay be admitted more frequently. It was reconsidered by The Law Commission in 1997 and Sir Robin Auld in 2001. He recommended a flexible approach. Sections 114–136 of the **Criminal Justice Act 2003** are intended to codify hearsay

law. They remove the old common law rule and provide that such evidence will be admissible provided certain safeguards are met. The court may allow an out-of-court statement where all parties agree, or it is satisfied that it is in the interests of justice for it to be admitted. Witnesses' previous statements are more widely admissible at trial, including DVD recorded statements in place of their main evidence, in serious trials.

4. *Confessions obtained by oppression* or in consequence of anything said or done which, in the circumstances, rendered the confession unreliable. The burden of proving that a confession was not so obtained is on the prosecution (Police and Criminal Evidence Act 1984 s.76).
5. *Unfairly obtained evidence* (**Police and Criminal Evidence Act 1984** s.78).

YOUNG OFFENDERS

The age of criminal responsibility is 10. Most 10–17 year old offenders are cautioned by the police following an admission of guilt. For those who are prosecuted, almost all are dealt with in the youth court, a court using a mixed gender bench or a district judge in the magistrates' court. The public are excluded. Journalists may report proceedings but not identify the young defendant or witnesses. Procedure is informal, normally without fixed court furniture. The magistrates or DJ(MC) address the defendant by first name and parents or guardians may accompany the child. Magistrates' disposal powers are different from those relating to adult offenders. Young offenders may only be sent for trial in the Crown Court if certain statutory conditions are satisfied, such as those under Sch.3 of the **Criminal Justice Act 2003**. For example, magistrates must send the following to the Crown Court:

- Children charged with murder, manslaughter or firearms offences.
- Children charged with adults.
- Children convicted in the magistrates' court, where the magistrates' court feels that they deserve a greater sentence than they can apply.

This is not a complete list. Rose L.J. described the procedure for determining a young person's mode of trial as "labyrinthine". For children tried in the Crown Court, the ECtHR has ruled that the normal adult trial is too intimidating and incomprehensible for a child and a breach of art.6: *T. and V. v UK* [2000] 2 All E.R. 1024. Consequently, the **Consolidated Criminal Practice Direction**, Pt IV says that youth trials must be conducted in accordance with the age, maturity and development of the defendant. Robes, wigs and police uniform should not normally be worn, the participants should be on the same floor level, the defendant should be able to sit near family or guardians, and should be given frequent breaks, and so on.

CRIMINAL APPEALS

There is no logic in our appeals system. For an excellent, thought-provoking examination, see J. Spencer, "Does Our Present Criminal Appeal System Make Sense?" [2006] Crim. L.R. 677 and Law Commission Consultation Paper No 184.

Appeals from the magistrates' court

Appeals to the Crown Court

A defendant may appeal, as of right, on fact or law and against sentence and/or conviction. The appeal is a complete rehearing by a circuit judge or recorder and two to four magistrates. The Crown Court may:

- correct any mistake in the order or judgment;
- confirm, reverse or vary the decision;
- remit the matter, with its opinion, to the magistrates; and
- make any order it thinks just and exercise any power of the magistrates' court. Thus, it may increase a sentence, within the magistrates' maxima.

Appeals to the High Court by way of case stated

Any prosecutor or defendant, aggrieved by the magistrates' decision, may, if they consider it wrong in law or in excess of jurisdiction, apply to the magistrates to state a case for the opinion of the HC. The stated case is a statement of reasons for the decision drafted by the magistrates' clerk (legal adviser). These appeals are heard by the Divisional Court of the Queen's Bench Division who may:

- reverse, affirm or amend the decision;
- remit it to the magistrates, with an opinion; or
- make such other orders as it thinks fit, including directing the magistrates to convict or acquit.

The QBD may also be asked to judicially review the magistrates' court proceedings on the ground of procedural impropriety, unfairness or bias, though the QBD has said it prefers the case stated procedure to be used. A further appeal, subject to leave, is permitted to the UKSC, as below.

Appeals from the Crown Court to the Court of Appeal (Criminal Division)

Appeal against conviction

Under the Criminal Appeal Act 1995 s.1, the convicted defendant may appeal if he has either:

- a certificate from the trial judge that the case is fit for appeal; or
- leave (permission) of the CA.

Single HC judges consider written applications for leave. Applicants have around a 25 per cent chance of success. Where leave is refused, the judge may order that time spent in custody after lodging the appeal should not count towards sentence. This is to discourage frivolous appeals, which burden the lists and delay meritorious appeals. The CA's powers are set out in the Criminal Appeal Act 1968, which has been substantially amended by the **1995 Act**. This section sets out the amended version of the **1968 Act** and then explains the background to the **1995 Act**.

The CA's power to admit fresh evidence

Under s.23 (1) and (3) of the **1968 Act**, as amended by the **1995 Act**, the CA may, *"if they think it necessary or expedient in the interests of justice"*,

(i) order the production of any *document*, exhibit or other thing connected with the proceedings;
(ii) order the examination of any *witness* who would have been a compellable witness at the trial, whether or not he or she was called; and
(iii) receive any *evidence* which was not adduced in the proceedings from which the appeal lies.

In considering whether to receive evidence, the CA must have regard in particular to:

"(a) whether the evidence appears to the court to be *capable of belief*;

(b) whether it appears to the court that the evidence may afford any *ground* for allowing the appeal;
(c) whether the evidence would have been *admissible* in the proceedings from which the appeal lies on an issue which is the subject of the appeal and
(d) whether there is a reasonable *explanation* for the failure to adduce the evidence in those proceedings"

The CA has held itself to be free to admit evidence irrespective of these criteria: *R. v Bowler* [1997] EWCA Crim 1957.

Background

Prior to 1995, the CA had a duty to admit fresh evidence where it was not available at the original trial, under prescribed conditions, and a wider power to admit it if it thought it necessary or expedient in the interests of justice. Its reluctance to admit fresh evidence was repeatedly criticised by the pressure group JUSTICE and by the producers of the television series *Rough Justice*, which focused on alleged miscarriages of justice. The CA required a particular type of explanation as to why evidence was not called at the time of trial, such as that it was not available. If it was available but simply not called, owing to, say, defence lawyers' negligence, prosecution's obstructiveness or a shortfall of legal aid, then this apparently would not suffice as an explanation acceptable to the CA. In many of these cases it took a "trial by television" and a reference by the Home Secretary to reopen the case. The House of Commons Home Affairs Committee in the early 1980s, then JUSTICE in 1989, then the RCCJ in 1993 urged the CA to take a broad approach to the question whether fresh evidence was available at the time of the trial and, if it were, to the explanation why it was not adduced or why a witness had changed his story. The test for receiving fresh evidence, argued the RCCJ, should be whether it was "capable of belief". In fresh evidence cases, the CA should order a retrial unless impracticable, in which case it should decide the case itself.

In a 1994 consultation paper, the Home Office broadly agreed but thought the CA's power to exclude fresh evidence should be preserved in cases where there was no reasonable explanation for the failure to produce it at trial. As you can see above, this is satisfied in the Act by the use of the word *may* in conjunction with its power to have regard to the explanation offered. In *Pendleton* [2001] UKHL 66, the leading case, the House of Lords said the correct test for the CA to apply was to consider the effect of the fresh evidence on the minds of the court, not the effect it would have had on a jury. In *R. v Gautier* [2007] All E.R. (D) 137, where the appellant sought to rely on a witness not called by the defendant's lawyer at the trial, the CA said it would not admit the new evidence unless there was a "lurking doubt", caused by flagrantly incompetent advocacy.

Grounds for allowing and dismissing appeals

Section 2 of the **Criminal Appeal Act 1968**, as amended, now provides that:

> "Subject to the provisions of this Act, the Court of Appeal
>
> (a) *shall* allow an appeal against conviction if they think that the conviction is unsafe; and
> (b) *shall* dismiss such an appeal in any other case". (My emphasis).

Background

Under the unamended **Criminal Appeal Act 1968**, the CA had the power to allow an appeal if it considered a jury's verdict "unsafe or unsatisfactory" or that there was an error of law or material irregularity in the course of the trial. Section 2 included a very important *proviso* which meant that the court could dismiss an appeal where, despite finding that something had gone wrong at the trial, it thought the defendant was, nevertheless, really guilty so that "no miscarriage of justice has actually occurred". The CA had been criticised for too readily using the proviso to uphold convictions where something had gone seriously wrong at the trial.

The RCCJ recommended that s.2 (1) of the **1968 Act** should be redrafted. It considered that the grounds overlapped and that there was confusion over the proviso. The grounds should be replaced by a single broad ground giving the CA power to rule in any case where it felt a conviction "is or may be unsafe". This power would be exercisable regardless of there being no fresh evidence, no error in law and no material irregularity. It recommended that the CA should have an additional power to refer cases that require further investigation to a new body for investigating alleged miscarriages of justice. This was established; the Criminal Cases Review Commission is described below. The Government broadly agreed but notice that the CA now has to be satisfied that the verdict *is* unsafe. The Royal Commission's suggested words "or may be" were not included. Critics have said that this is too restrictive on the CA's powers. As well as the power to quash a conviction, the CA also has the power to order a retrial, or convict for an alternative offence, or substitute a verdict of insanity or unfitness to plead.

The Court of Appeal's attitude towards its powers

Generally speaking, the CA was criticised pre-1995 for placing too restrictive an interpretation on its already limited powers. The main reason why the CA is so reluctant to overturn a conviction by a Crown Court jury is that, unlike the jury, it has not seen the witnesses and evidence first-hand. Further, it tends to revere the primacy of the jury, as the quotation below illustrates.

KEY POINT

It is important to understand that the CA does not provide a rehearing in criminal cases, unlike an appeal from a magistrates' court to the Crown Court. The limited powers of the CA were spelled out in the successful 1991 appeal of the Birmingham Six, *R. v McIlkenny* [1992] 2 All E.R. 417:

> "Nothing in s.2 of the Act, or anywhere else obliges or entitles us to say whether we think that the appellant is innocent. This is a point of great constitutional importance. The task of deciding whether a man is innocent or guilty falls on the jury. We are concerned solely with the question whether the verdict of the jury can stand. Rightly or wrongly (we think rightly) trial by jury is the foundation of our criminal justice system . . . The primacy of the jury in the criminal justice system is well illustrated by the difference between the Criminal and Civil Divisions of the Court of Appeal . . . A civil appeal is by way of rehearing of the whole case. So the court is concerned with fact as well as law . . . It follows that in a civil case the Court of Appeal may take a different view of the facts from the court below. In a criminal case this is not possible . . . the Criminal Division is perhaps more accurately described as a court of review" (at 311).

The CA is continually swamped with criminal appeals and there are so many decisions on the meaning of "unsafe" that it is not possible to generalise. In *R. v A* [2001] UKHL 25, the House of Lords (law lords) held that a breach of **art.6** of the **European Convention** will always result in a conviction being unsafe. In *R. v Ashton* [2006] EWCA Crim 794 the CA took a very restricted attitude to allowing a conviction to be quashed where there had been a procedural failure but there was no real possibility that the prosecution or defence had been prejudiced by it. These cases follow a trend in which the court seemed to be attempting to put a stop to people "getting off on a technicality". They shift concentration to the individual justice of a case. The

CA sometimes allows an appeal on the rather vague old common law ground that they have a "lurking doubt" about the safety of a conviction. See *Leigh* at [2006] Crim. L.R. 809.

The power to order retrials

The **1968 Act** s.7, as amended by the **Criminal Justice Act 1988**, provides that, where the CA allows an appeal against conviction, it may order that the appellant be retried where it appears that this is required in the interests of justice.

Appeals against sentence and Att Gen's references on sentence

The defendant may appeal from the Crown Court to the CA, which may substitute any other sentence or order within the powers of the Crown Court, provided it is not more severe than originally. The **Criminal Justice Act 1988** s.36 gives the Att Gen a power to refer any "unduly lenient" Crown Court sentence to the CA, which then has the power to increase it. The Att Gen may then refer any such decision of the CA to the UK Supreme Court.

Prosecution appeals: Attorney General's References

The Att Gen may, under the **Criminal Justice Act 1972**, refer an appeal, following an acquittal, to the CA and UKSC, on behalf of the prosecution. The appeal court simply clarifies the law, leaving the acquittal untouched.

Prosecution appeals against a trial judge's ruling

The **Criminal Justice Act 2003** Pt 9 introduced a right of appeal to the CA by the prosecution against a judge's ruling (usually on a point of law or admissibility or strength of the evidence) which has terminated the trial (thus acquitting the accused) before a jury has been convened or during the prosecution case, or as a result of a submission of "no case to answer" by the defence, at the conclusion of the prosecution case. The Act also introduced a prosecution appeal against a judge's ruling which has been made at any time before the close of the prosecution case. In both instances, the prosecution must obtain leave from the trial judge or the CA. The CA may affirm the ruling and acquit the defendant, remit the case to the trial court for the trial to continue or order a retrial. This follows a recommendation by Auld L.J. in the Criminal Courts Review 2001, agreeing with recommendations of the Law Commission.

Prosecution applications to quash an acquittal

The **2003 Act** Pt 10 also made a controversial exception to the double jeopardy rule, which protects a person from being tried twice for the same offence. With the DPP's consent, a prosecutor may apply to the CA to quash an acquittal and order a retrial. If the CA is satisfied that there is "new and compelling evidence" (reliable, substantial and highly probative) against the acquitted person, in relation to the offence, and that it is in the interests of justice to do so, it *must* quash the acquittal and order a retrial. The provision applies only to serious offences such as rape, armed robbery, murder and manslaughter. This follows a recommendation of Auld L.J. *R. v Dunlop* [2006] EWCA Crim 1354 was the first time the CA exercised this power, quashing Dunlop's 1991 acquittal for the murder of Julie Hogg. He confessed to the murder in 1999. This case was well known and highly publicised at the time that Auld L.J. made his 2001 recommendation. Dunlop pleaded guilty at his retrial in 2006.

Appeals to the UK Supreme Court

Either prosecutor or defendant may appeal, with leave, to the UKSC, from an appeal hearing in the Divisional Court of the High Court QBD, on a *point of law of general public importance* (**Administration of Justice Act 1960**). This is called a "leapfrog" appeal, because the case by-passes the CA. Either prosecutor or defendant may appeal from the CA, provided the CA certifies that a point of law of general public importance is involved and that either court considers that the point should be considered by the UKSC and grants leave. The UKSC, in disposing of the appeal, may exercise any of the powers of the CA, or remit the case to it (**Criminal Appeal Act 1968**).

THE POST-APPEAL STAGE: RE-EXAMINING ALLEGED MISCARRIAGES OF JUSTICE

Where a person thinks he has been wrongly convicted by a jury or magistrates, and he has lost an appeal or been refused leave to appeal, he may now seek the assistance of the independent Criminal Cases Review Commission (CCRC), or somebody else may petition them on his behalf. This is likely to be an M.P., or a campaigning group, or an organisation such as JUSTICE. The CCRC was created by the **1995 Act**. Its 11 members are appointed for five years. One third must be legally qualified.

1. The CCRC is empowered to refer Crown Court convictions and sentences to the CA and summary convictions and sentences (made by the magistrates' court) to the Crown Court.
2. It must "consider that there is a real possibility that the conviction, verdict, finding or sentence would not be upheld, were the reference to be made" because of argument or evidence not raised earlier. These conditions appear rather restrictive but these are followed by a broad power to make a reference "if it appears to the Commission that there are exceptional circumstances which justify making it".
3. It may not refer a conviction back to the CA just because the law has changed: **Criminal Justice and Immigration Act 2008** s.42.
4. It may be directed by the CA to investigate a case and
5. may be asked by the Home Secretary to consider a matter arising in his consideration of whether to exercise the prerogative of mercy.
6. The CCRC has powers to obtain documents and may direct investigations by police officers or another public body.

Although the CCRC is a welcome replacement for the former arrangements for investigating alleged miscarriages of justice (a handful of Home Office civil servants), the CCRC's powers and approach have been criticised. It has always had a backlog of thousands of cases awaiting investigation, which is not alleviated by its preparedness to spend time re-examining the cases of those long dead. Some critics, such as Duff, have said that the CCRC is preoccupied with trying to second guess the CA. He thought they should more readily refer cases to the Home Secretary in the hope that he will exercise his prerogative of mercy. For statistics and details of its caseload see the CCRC website and for a debate on the success rate and working methods of the CCRC, see Nobles and Schiff's critique at [2005] Crim. L.R. 173 and reply by the then CCRC chair, Graham Zellick at [2005] Crim. L.R. 237.

The royal prerogative of mercy

The prerogative of mercy is the power to pardon convicted individuals as part of the residuary royal prerogative, exercised by the Crown on the advice of the Home Secretary. The prerogative is exercised in three ways:

(a) A free pardon: quashing and expunging a conviction.
(b) A conditional pardon: excusing or varying the conviction, subject to conditions, e.g. by commuting sentences.
(c) Remission of a sentence.

General background to the Criminal Appeal Act 1995: widespread concern over miscarriages of justice

Prior to 1995, the Home Secretary had both a prerogative power of mercy, which she retains, and a statutory power to refer cases to the CA. The Home Secretary always used the prerogative to pardon sparingly so as not to invoke the criticism of over-interference by the executive in the judicial function and because of the notion that the jury's verdict is sacrosanct. The House of Commons Home Affairs Committee complained in 1981 that the prerogative was used reluctantly. It recommended an independent review body. The RCCJ repeated that call.

The most famous miscarriages of justice in modern times are the cases of the Guildford Four and the Birmingham Six. The RCCJ was established to investigate the criminal justice process on the day the latter were released in 1991. Concerns had, however, been raised for decades beforehand, over individuals who had allegedly been wrongfully imprisoned. Television programmes such as *Rough Justice* had alerted the public to the inadequacy of the appeal and post-appeal procedures. These are probably best summarised in a JUSTICE Report, *Miscarriages of Justice* (1989). It is well worth reading and, below, I list the causes of injustice identified by their report, explaining, in square brackets, how these were later manifested in famous cases.

Pre-trial

1. Poor work by defence lawyers.
2. Cases involving poor police investigation and/or police misconduct. [The stories behind the Guildford Four and Birmingham Six involve a sad litany of police corruption, notably of police brutality inducing false confessions. *Downing* [2002] EWCA Crim 263 was a case where a vulnerable youngster confessed after oppressive detention, as was that of Robert Brown, freed on appeal in 2002, after 25 years in prison and Stephan Kisko, who wrongly confessed to a murder after two days' questioning, without a lawyer, and served 16 years of wrongful imprisonment.] The JUSTICE Report recites psychiatric research which gives a fascinating insight into why people confess to crimes they did not commit but for more detail see G. Gudjonsson, *The Psychology of Interrogations and Confessions: A Handbook* (2002).

Trial

3. Poor work by defence counsel: late briefs, bad trial tactics and failure to call witnesses.
4. Underhand tactics by the prosecution. [In the Guildford Four case, it

was alleged that the police realised, early on, that they might not have caught the right people but they suppressed evidence in favour of the defence, such as an interview with an alibi witness.]

5. Poor summing up by the judge. [In the Guildford Four case, the summing up by the trial judge was acknowledged by the CA to be faulty but it did not consider it sufficient reason to allow leave to appeal. As for the Birmingham Six, the summing up by their trial judge (who later became a law lord) went overboard in indicating a guilty verdict.]

Appeal

6. Bad advice on appeal.
7. The majority of appeals are concerned with legal technicalities, not the guilt or innocence of the accused.
8. A reluctance to interfere with the trial verdict. [In the Birmingham Six case, the CA, headed by Lord Lane C.J., which heard the Six's 1987 appeal, was very heavily criticised for its refusal to overturn the jury's verdict, despite new evidence casting serious doubt on the convictions.]

Post-appeal

9. The desire of former Home Secretaries, as part of the executive government, not to be seen to be interfering with the work of the courts led them to ignore errors 1–7 above. [By the time the Home Secretary had referred the Birmingham Six's appeal back to the CA, the case had already been the subject of a book and a TV drama documentary, and opinion polls showed that most Americans, including President Bush senior and most Irish people, including their Prime Minister, assumed the Six to be innocent.]
10. Inadequate re-investigation by the police. [The police were criticised for taking two years to investigate the Guildford Four's convictions.]

Additionally, the above cases and later cases, such as those of Sally Clark and Angela Cannings in 2003, highlighted specific weaknesses in the system:

11. Inefficiency in forensic science services and inadequate services for the defence, as emphasised by the May Inquiry into the Guildford and Maguire cases.
12. Inadequate safeguards for defendants held under terrorist legislation. [Note: many commentators have said the injustices occurring in the

Irish cases could not now be repeated because of the **Police and Criminal Evidence Act 1984**. This is erroneous. Today, suspected terrorists are still held under different statutory powers.]

13. The danger of allowing the jury to convict on uncorroborated confession evidence.
14. Over-anxiety on the part of the police to secure a conviction, including a preparedness to fabricate evidence, in cases where there is a public outcry against the perpetrators. All these cases involve Irish or black defendants.
15. Over-willingness in certain CA judges, pre-1990, to believe prosecution evidence, probably caused by the fact that the majority of them were recruited from prosecuting counsel. This is not true now.
16. Limited powers of the CA: an inability to provide a full rehearing.
17. Failure to disclose exculpatory evidence and over-reliance on individual expert evidence [such as in Sally Clark's and Angela Cannings' convictions for murder after their babies died. After these two cases, the CA laid down guidance to prosecutors in cot death cases (*Cannings* [2004] EWCA Crim 1) and the Att Gen reviewed over 258 convictions in similar cases. In his 2001 Review, Auld L.J. had expressed concern over the lack of regulation of experts. The Att Gen has published guidance for experts and see *R. v B* (CA 2006)].

THE EFFECT OF THE HUMAN RIGHTS ACT 1998 AND THE EUROPEAN CONVENTION ON HUMAN RIGHTS ON CRIMINAL PROCEDURE

The **Human Rights Act 1998** gave "further effect" to the **Convention** and required courts and tribunals to take it into account in their proceedings (this permits them to re-interpret the law and read words into a statute). Since 2000, when it came into force, the Act's biggest area of impact has been criminal procedure, notably via arts 5 and 6, above. Defendants can make use of the **Convention** in various ways, such as a defence, or to found an argument of "no case to answer", or as grounds of appeal. Below are some examples of the **Convention**'s application. For an excellent two-page evaluation of the impact of the **HRA** on the criminal process see I. Dennis, Editorial: "Reconsidering the Human Rights Act" [2006] Crim. L.R. 577.

- Article 8 guarantees the right to private life, allowing interference only where necessary if national security and public safety are threatened, or in the prevention of crime and disorder. Surveillance methods, such as phone tapping and bugging must be prescribed by law, with a system of accountability. Liberty, the human rights organisation, and police organisations argue that this evidence should be used to try terrorist suspects, as it is throughout Europe, rather than detaining them in house arrest. Unusually, such evidence was used in the retrial of terrorists in 2009, convicted of plotting to blow up aircraft using bombs disguised as soft drinks. In 2009, the Home Office consulted on *Keeping the Right People on the DNA Database*, after the ECtHR ruled that the policy of indefinite retention of arrested people's fingerprints breached art. 8.

- Article 6(3)(c) (fair trial) grants the right to legal assistance to everyone charged with a criminal offence where it is "necessary in the interests of justice"; this is the criterion for publicly-funded defence, set out in the **Access to Justice Act 1999**. The ECtHR has held that an accused's right to communicate in confidence with his lawyer is an essential element of art.6 (3)(c).
- In *SS for the Home Dept v AF and another* [2009] UKHL 28, the law lords ruled that the appellant's art.6 fair trial rights had been violated as he had been the subject of a control order (house arrest), as a terror suspect, pursuant to the **Terrorism Act 2005** s.2, for three years. The government sought non-disclosure of intelligence on which the house arrest was based. Rather than disclose the evidence and jeopardise other terror investigations, the Home Secretary lifted the order.
- The law and practice on bail had to be amended, to make it **Convention**-compliant, as explained above. Courts now need more substantial evidence on which to base their bail decisions. They must keep them under review and they must keep in mind the presumption of innocence, and give full reasons, not just "tick-box" reasons. A statute banning bail for certain suspects had to be amended as it breached the **Convention.**
- As explained above, in the section on the right of silence, after *Saunders*, various statutes had to be amended by the **Youth Justice and Criminal Evidence Act 1999** because they required a suspect to answer questions and thus fell foul of art.6.
- Critics said the statutory regime for disclosure under the **Criminal Procedure and Investigations Act 1996** fell foul of art.6 in various ways and it has now been amended in the **Criminal Justice Act 2003**, as explained.
- The ECtHR has held that a costs order against an acquitted defendant violates the presumption of innocence, under art.6(2).
- The child murderers of Jamie Bulger took the UK Government to the ECtHR, alleging they had been denied a fair trial under art.6 (*T and V v UK* (2000) 30 E.H.R.R. 121). The Court agreed that the formality and

ritual of the Crown Court trial must have been intimidating and incomprehensible to 11-year-old children. Consequently, Crown Court youth trial practice was reformed, as explained.

- The **Convention** requires a reasoned decision. Nevertheless, in *Gregory v UK* (1998) 25 E.H.R.R. 577, the ECtHR held that the secrecy of jury deliberations did not render a trial unfair. Magistrates' courts are not courts of record. Historically this made appeals difficult. Magistrates now keep trial notes and give reasoned decisions.
- In *Sander v UK* (2001) 31 E.H.R.R. 44 the ECtHR ruled that the defendant's fraud trial had been in breach of art.6 because one of the jurors had warned the judge that the jury might not be impartial because some of them were making racist jokes.
- English and Welsh judges are extremely reluctant to allow handcuffs in court: art.3, prohibition of torture, inhuman or degrading treatment.

Revision Checklist

You need to appreciate the following points and understand any arguments surrounding them.

- The importance of the common law and **European Convention on Human Rights** as the basis for criminal procedure rules, and the relationship between them.
- The main case management elements and ethos of the **Criminal Procedure Rules.**
- Prosecutors and how the prosecution system works.
- How the bail system works and the grounds for refusing bail.
- How legislation has affected the right to silence, the controversy surrounding this, and how the European Court of Human Rights has ruled on this issue.
- How cases are allocated between the magistrates' court and the Crown Court and the arguments for and against retaining the defendant's right to choose the mode of trial (right to elect jury trial).
- The rules of pre-trial disclosure and how these have been altered in 2003.
- The system of rewarding guilty pleas, unofficially called "plea bargaining"; how informal sentencing rewards have now been sanctioned by the law and how practice has now been set down by **Goodyear** and the Sentencing Council.

- The pre-trial hearings that may take place, the basic pattern of civil and criminal trials, and the special safeguards in the criminal trial.
- The system of criminal appeals and how this was reformed in the **Criminal Appeal Act 1995.**
- The system for dealing with alleged miscarriages of justice at the post-appeal stage and the common causes of miscarriages of justice.
- The way in which the **European Convention on Human Rights** and its interpretation by the European Court of Human Rights has impacted on criminal procedure and practice in England and Wales.

CHANGING AND "REFORMING" CRIMINAL PROCEDURE

Criminal procedure is complex and fast changing. It is highly political because governments want to be seen to be responding to crime. Policy plans are published in white papers. The latest is the July 2012 *Swift and Sure Justice*. Apart from proposals discussed above and in Chapter 3 on the court structure, it proposed permitting individual lay magistrates to deal with some uncontested, low-level crime on their own. The paper promises to reduce bureaucracy, complaining that it takes about 53 steps and 17 weeks to prosecute a common assault case. The Government is trying to introduce digital working in the criminal courts. Given that this did not succeed in the civil courts, the outcome remains to be seen.

FURTHER READING/UPDATING

Darbyshire on the ELS (2011), Chapter 12, further reading listed therein and website updates
Archbold News (on *Westlaw*)
Criminal Law Review (on *Westlaw*)
New Law Journal
Legal Journals Index (on *Westlaw*)

websites

Attorney General
Criminal Cases Review Commission

Criminal Courts Review
Crown Prosecution Service
HM Courts and Tribunals Service
Ministry of Justice, especially Criminal Procedure Rules and the Consolidated Criminal Practice Direction
Youth Justice Board

QUESTION AND ANSWER

The Question

Priya is arrested for theft of a bar of chocolate from her local convenience store. (Theft is an "either way" offence). Explain what may happen to her and the choices that she may be faced with.

Advice and the Answer

Advice

This is a problem. Deal with the problem. Do not write all you know about criminal procedure or lapse into a discursive essay about it. Do not get bogged down in writing in detail about part of the procedure because you need to provide a balanced account. Describe it in outline then expand as time allows. In an exam, leave a few lines before each point, to allow room for elaboration, or in case you remember something you have missed out.

Answer guide

1. If Priya admits her guilt to the police, she may be dealt with by an early intervention scheme or may be offered a caution, instead of prosecution. A caution will go on her criminal record. A caution is highly likely, if she is 10–17, since most offences committed by young offenders are disposed of by way of a caution, meaning a reprimand or final warning, under the **Crime and Disorder Act 1998**, unless she is a persistent offender. If she is an adult, she may still be offered a caution, or a conditional caution under the **CJA 2003**. A child or adult may be dealt with by a fixed penalty, imposed by the police. This does not form part of the offender's criminal record but police and courts do have access to records of fixed penalties.

2. In taking this important decision, she should be offered the assistance of the duty solicitor, or may apply for a solicitor of her choice, under the legal aid scheme, if she cannot afford to pay privately. If she is a child, she will not be means tested. As a child or adult, her case will still have to satisfy the "interests of justice" test and she is more likely to satisfy it if she is a child because she will be less capable of representing herself.
3. If she is under ten, she is below the age of criminal responsibility and may not be treated as a criminal suspect, though the police will no doubt inform and warn her parent(s) or guardian(s). If an adult told her to steal, she is their innocent agent and *they* may be charged with theft.
4. If not cautioned, the police or prosecutor may decide to charge her with theft. The Crown Prosecution Service will apply the Code for Crown Prosecutors in deciding whether to proceed with the prosecution.
5. They will apply the evidential sufficiency test first. If there is insufficient evidence against her—for instance, no eyewitness or security camera evidence and she was not caught red-handed—they may decide not to prosecute.
6. If that test is satisfied, however, they will go on to apply the public interest test. For example, if she is found to be terminally ill or if she is very old and also senile, or has severe learning difficulties, they may decide that the public interest factors against a prosecution outweigh the factors in favour.
7. If the CPS declines to prosecute, the store may prosecute her or take a civil action against her, which would be much easier to prove, because of the lower degree of proof.
8. If prosecuted, she is highly unlikely to be remanded.
9. She will be summoned to appear in the magistrates' court as soon as possible.
10. If she is 10–17, she will appear before the youth court, a closed court, comprising mixed-gender lay magistrates or a DJMC. She will not be given the choice of a jury trial in the Crown Court and the magistrates will not send her to trial in the Crown Court, unless charged with an adult, because the alleged crime is not sufficiently grave. The press may attend the youth court and report but may not identify her. Her parents/guardians will be strongly encouraged to accompany her and the magistrates will strongly encourage her to take legal advice from the duty solicitor, if she is not already accompanied by a solicitor. If she pleads guilty, the bench may sentence her there and then, or

request a report. If she pleads not guilty, there will be a trial, usually adjourned until a later date. If the bench are not satisfied of guilt beyond reasonable doubt, they must acquit her. If they find the case proven, they will convict her. They may sentence her immediately if convicted, or require a report on her by a social worker, before sentencing. Under certain circumstances, the bench may impose a referral order, in which case she will be referred to the local Youth Offending Panel.

11. If she is an adult, she will appear before the next magistrates' court and the magistrates will take her plea before determining mode of trial. She may be advised and/or represented by the duty solicitor or a privately paid for barrister or solicitor. She may qualify for legal aid if she satisfies the means test and the interests of justice test. She will satisfy the interests of justice test if, for example, she is in danger of losing liberty or livelihood, if convicted, or if she needs an interpreter, or if she lacks full mental capacity or is in some other way vulnerable. If she is granted publicly funded help, she may be required to make contributions towards the cost. The magistrates will take account of her plea and criminal record and the allocation guidelines in determining whether to accept jurisdiction or send her up to the Crown Court for trial. They are highly unlikely to do so, whatever her plea. In this case, the choice of court then falls to her and she can ask the magistrates for an advance indication of sentence in aiding her choice, but they do not have to give one.
12. If she is an adult, pleading guilty, the DJMC or magistrates may sentence her immediately, after a brief plea in mitigation, or they may adjourn for a pre-sentence report or medical or psychiatric report, if necessary.
13. If she pleads not guilty and is content to be tried by the magistrates, a bench of three or a DJMC, advised by a legal adviser, will try her later, in an adjourned hearing, to give prosecution and defence time to prepare the case. The bench will decide on guilt or innocence and then, with the advice of their legal adviser, will sentence her.
14. If she pleads not guilty and opts to be tried at the Crown Court, she is likely to be bailed to appear at a later date, while the case is transferred. Her solicitor will brief a barrister to represent her, unless the solicitor has an advocacy certificate granting rights of audience in the Crown Court. As above, she may be granted publicly funded representation.

15. At the Crown Court, she may appear at a plea and case management hearing. If she changes her plea to guilty, she may be sentenced by the judge or recorder as soon as he has the benefit of a pre-sentence report. If she maintains her plea of not guilty, the judge will fix the trial date and make other arrangements for the trial. Any further hearing, requiring her presence, may not be necessary if everything is organised by the case progression officer. (Points on case management may be expanded.)
16. If she maintains her not guilty plea, the prosecutor or her defence team may enter plea negotiations. She may be offered a sentence discount in exchange for an immediate guilty plea. (This point can be expanded.)
17. If, however, she maintains her not guilty plea, she will be tried by a jury of 12, who will determine guilt or innocence and the trial will be conducted by a circuit judge or recorder, who will control procedure, determine points of law, sum up the evidence to the jury and instruct them on law.
18. At any time pre-trial or during the trial, the judge may order or direct an acquittal on a point of law or evidential sufficiency and the prosecution may appeal to the CA against such a ruling.
19. If she is found guilty by the jury, she will be sentenced by the recorder or judge.
20. If she is found not guilty, she will be acquitted and discharged. The prosecution may appeal, with leave, to the CA on a point of law, which will not affect her acquittal, or against an unduly lenient sentence, in which case the CA may increase her sentence.
21. If she has been convicted in the magistrates' court, she has an unfettered right to appeal against sentence and/or conviction to the Crown Court, where the appeal will be heard by a recorder or judge with two lay justices. If appealing against conviction, there will be a full rehearing. If she feels the magistrates' have erred on law or exceeded their jurisdiction, she may ask them to state a case (give fuller reasons) and appeal by way of case stated to the Divisional Court of the QBD. This court may quash her conviction or uphold it or remit it to the magistrates, with a direction. If she has been acquitted by magistrates, the prosecutor may appeal by way of case stated, on the same grounds. Either party may apply to the Div Court for a judicial review of the case, if they consider there was a procedural irregularity (e.g. alleged bias), or the magistrates exceeded their

jurisdiction or acted unreasonably. The losing side may, with leave, appeal to the CA on a point of law, or, with leave, "leapfrog" to the UKSC, if the case is certified as raising a point of law of general public importance.

22. If she has been convicted in the Crown Court she may seek leave to appeal to the CA against conviction and/or sentence. She is likely to be refused leave and may renew her application before the CA in person. If the CA considers her conviction is unsafe, they will quash it. They may reduce her sentence.
23. The losing party in the CA may apply for leave to appeal to the UKSC, and leave may be granted, provided the CA or UKSC also certifies that the case raises a point of law of general public importance. If the case raises a point of EU law, any court may refer it to the Court of Justice of the EU for a preliminary ruling and the CA or UKSC must refer, if they are the last court of appeal. If the case raises a human rights point, for instance over the right of silence, she may challenge the UK before the ECtHR.
24. If she has exhausted her rights of appeal and considers she has been wrongly convicted, she or anyone acting on her behalf may petition the CCRC, who, if they are convinced of a real possibility that the sentence or conviction would not be upheld, or in exceptional circumstances, may refer her conviction to the Crown Court if she was convicted in the magistrates' court, or to the CA, if she was convicted in the Crown Court.
25. If the court allows such an appeal, she may apply for statutory compensation for her wrongful conviction.
26. In addition to the points above, mention could be made of her right of silence, bail issues, the rules on pre-trial disclosure in the Crown Court and judges' rulings on a point of law and appeals against such rulings. The point on plea negotiations could have been expanded. Mention could have been made of a possible retrial following an acquittal resulting from a hung jury.

Lawyers

7

INTRODUCTION

KEY POINT

Unlike most legal professions, the English and Welsh one is divided into two main groups, solicitors and barristers, which were traditionally characterised by their monopolies. The Bar had a monopoly over rights of audience (rights to argue a case) in the higher courts and solicitors had a monopoly over direct contact with most clients, conveyancing (transfer) of property, litigation (preparing a civil case, pre-trial) and probate (administration of a dead person's property). These monopolies were eroded in the 1980s and '90s and the legal profession has been in a state of flux since it was the subject of scrutiny by the Royal Commission on Legal Services (RCLS) 1979. The 2004 Clementi proposals to restructure the legal profession resulted in the **Legal Services Act 2007** (LSA 2007). This changed the way lawyers are regulated but also permitted new types of business structure with mixed firms of lawyers and other professionals, and permitted law firms to be owned by, or operate through, other commercial organisations. The first high street brand to offer legal services under this regime is the Co-op. In the meantime, while the main legal professions have been squabbling since 1980 about their monopolies and restrictive practices, over 300,000 paralegals have sneaked up behind them, in 6,500 paralegal law firms, offering every day legal services.

This chapter examines the following topics.

- Organisation and regulatory structure.
- Numbers of barristers and solicitors and diversity issues.
- Legal education.
- The dismantling of monopolies and restrictive practices
- The Clementi Report and the resultant **Legal Services Act 2007**.
- The impact of the Act and other factors on lawyers' business structures and their work.
- Arguments for and against fusion.

LEGAL SERVICES ACT 2007

It created a new regulatory structure, the objects of which are:

- protecting and promoting public interest;
- supporting the rule of law;
- improving access to justice;
- protecting consumer interests;
- promoting competition in legal services;
- encouraging an independent, strong, diverse and effective legal profession;
- increasing public understanding of citizens' rights and duties; and
- promoting professional principles.

All the representative and regulatory bodies described below are under a duty to promote these objects.

The Legal Services Board (LSB) and the Legal Ombudsman

The LSB was created by the **2007 Act** to oversee the eight bodies regulating different types of lawyer, including solicitors. The Legal Ombudsman was created under the Act, in 2010, and is a free complaints service about the main categories of lawyer or legal service provider: barristers, law costs draftsmen, legal executives, licensed conveyancers, notaries, patent attorneys, probate practitioners, registered European lawyers, solicitors, and trademark attorneys.

SOLICITORS

Structure, organisation and regulation

In 2011, there were 159,524 solicitors on the Roll, 121,933 of whom had practising certificates in private practice, and the remainder of whom worked in commerce or the public sector. The Law Society's Annual Statistical Reports, *Trends in the Solicitors' Profession*, are on its website.

The Law Society

This is the trade union of solicitors, to "help, protect and promote solicitors across England and Wales" (website). It used to be the professional regulatory body but lost this function under the **2007 Act**.

The Solicitors Regulation Authority (SRA)

This is the professional governing body of solicitors, regulating their training, discipline and standards of professional conduct. It can fine individuals and law firms and/or apply conditions to their authorisation and refer them to the Solicitors Disciplinary Tribunal, which can levy unlimited fines.

The Office of Legal Complaints

Since 2010, this impartial body handles complaints. The function was removed from the Law Society by the **2007 Act**.

Gender balance

In 2011, women accounted for 46.5 per cent of solicitors with practising certificates, representing a growth of 80 per cent since 2001. Almost 60 per cent of newly admitted solicitors were women. Women do not progress as readily as men. Despite the fact that 59 per cent of new solicitors in 2011 were women, in 2010 *The Times* reported that women comprised fewer than 20 per cent of partners in Britain's 30 biggest law firms. The Law Society has long been concerned with the drop-out rate, reflected in the fact that in 2011, the average male private practitioner was 45 and the average female about 38. The Law Society exposed a 32 per cent median pay gap in 2008. Half of 800 women solicitors surveyed by the Law Society in 2010 feared their career prospects would suffer if they made use of family friendly policies. More optimistically, C. McConnell demonstrated how the regulatory objectives of the **2007 Act** could be used to benefit women and minority solicitors. She quoted the 2009–10 business plan of the LSB to "promote equality". (2009) 159 N.L.J. 863.

Ethnicity and social diversity

The RCLS 1979 found discrimination. It deprecated the formation of minority firms of solicitors and barristers' chambers. In 1986, the Law Society belatedly established an ethnic monitoring scheme and a Race Relations Committee. In 2011, 12 per cent of solicitors were from ethnic minorities, as were 22 per cent of students enrolling with the Law Society but the biggest problem they face lies in entering the profession and progressing to partnerships. The Law Society and governments have introduced many initiatives since the 1980s to promote diversity. The Society conducted three surveys in 2010 on barriers faced by minorities. A 2008 salary survey demonstrated a pay gap between whites and non-whites. BME solicitors considered that they had been channelled towards legally aided work, which was less lucrative than company and commercial work. In 2009, the Cabinet Office published

Unleashing Aspiration, which disclosed that half of professional occupations are dominated by those from public schools.

BARRISTERS

Structure and organisation

In 2010 there were 15,378 barristers with practising certificates, 80 per cent of whom were in private practice, distributed between 330 sets of chambers, most of which were in London. 419 worked as sole practitioners. There were over 2,967 employed barristers. The Bar has grown considerably since 1960 when there were only 1,919 practising barristers but growth has slowed significantly in recent years. Statistics are on the Bar Council website, in *Bar Barometer*.

The Bar Council

The General Council of the Bar represents the interests of barristers. It was their professional governing body but lost that function to the Bar Standards Board in advance of the **LSA 2007**. The six court circuits have their own Bar Associations, as do specialist barristers.

The Inns of Court

Each barrister must belong to an Inn of Court: Gray's Inn, Lincoln's Inn, Inner Temple or Middle Temple. Historically, they had a collegiate function. They educated students in the common law which was practised in the courts, because the universities only taught civil (Roman) law.

The Bar Standards Board

This was created in 2006, anticipating the **LSA 2007**, taking over enforcement of professional standards and enforcing the Bar's Code of Conduct. It handles complaints and is subject to oversight by the LSB, above.

Professional Liability

In 2000 in *Arthur JS Hall (a firm) v Simons* [2002] 1 A.C. 615, the House of Lords held that barristers and other advocates (including solicitors) could be sued for negligence in their conduct of civil and criminal proceedings. This reversed the old rule in *Rondel v Worsley* [1969] 1 A.C. 191.

The Bar's archaic practising arrangements

Chambers

Until 1990, every practising barrister had to rent a "tenancy" (really a subtenancy) in a "set" of "chambers" (meaning offices—note the archaic language) and until the 1980s most London chambers had to be within the Inns of Court. The growth of the Bar led to derestriction. Barristers of three years' call may now practise independently. Securing a "tenancy" is very difficult and the number of tenancies decreased by over three per cent per year in 2005–10. Under the **LSA 2007**, barristers may join legal disciplinary practices and alternative business structures, explained below. What proportion of barristers will do so is unpredictable, though early research indicated that the majority would not.

The clerk

Most "sets" have one chief clerk, or practice manager, and several juniors. All barristers must obtain their work and negotiate fees via the clerk. Historically, it was thought unseemly for barristers to do this, hence the pocket on the back of the gown, to receive the solicitor's *honorarium*, "gift for services rendered".

The hierarchy

The top nine per cent or so of barristers are called Queen's Counsel, more commonly called "silks", as they are entitled to wear a silk gown instead of a stuff gown. All other barristers are known as "junior barristers". QCs take the most serious cases, charging high fees. They are appointed by the Crown. They used to be selected by the Lord Chancellor (L.C.) but, following criticism that the system was discriminatory and anti-competitive, the annual "silk" competition since 2005–06 is organised by a company run by the Law Society and the Bar. There used to be a rule called the Two Counsel Rule whereby each QC had to pay a junior to appear with them in court. This rule was abolished in 1977 but it is still widely followed in practice. It was the subject of repeated scrutiny and in 2000 the Lord Chancellor further restricted the use of silk or more than one advocate, in publicly funded Crown Court cases. Solicitor advocates may be appointed as QCs but solicitors continue to complain about the QC system and want it abolished. See below.

Partnerships

Barristers generally stand or fall by their own individual skills (and health).

Until 2009, they were not allowed to form partnerships except if practising overseas but this rule had to change because of the new business structures permitted by the **LSA 2007**.

Pupillage

Barristers are qualified as soon as they are "called to the Bar", on passing the Bar Finals but, if they wish to practise, they must do a one-year pupillage. They accompany their "pupil-master" barrister, or work in another "approved training organisation". They can earn fees by taking cases on their own account in their second six months but having to support themselves in their first six was one of the factors which made going to the Bar so expensive. The Bar therefore provided for pupillage funding from 2002.

Rules of etiquette and unwritten rules

These seem designed to mark out the Bar as an elite, relative to solicitors and clients, and many members of the public wrongly assume that barristers are more highly qualified than solicitors, who continually complain of the arrogance of barristers. These are some of the best known:

- Barristers wear 18th century-style, male, horse-hair wigs in the Crown Court and some of the senior courts. Solicitor advocates were only allowed to wear wigs from 2008.
- In the courtroom, "silks" occupy the front row, nearest the judge, with junior barristers behind them and solicitors' representatives behind them. The exception is the solicitor-advocate, who is allowed to sit in the same row as the barrister.
- The judicial hierarchy reflects lawyers' hierarchy. Most senior judges were QCs. Most district judges were solicitors.

Gender

The RCLS 1979 found that over 90 sets of chambers contained no women. Astonishingly, gender and race discrimination at the Bar were not outlawed until the passage of the **Courts and Legal Services Act 1990** and, by the late 1990s, there were still sets of chambers with few or no women or minorities. The proportion of women as practising barristers is increasing slightly (32 and 46 per cent of self-employed and employed barristers, respectively, in 2010).

Ethnicity and Social Diversity

Black barristers complained that racism was institutionalised at the Bar. The RCLS 1979 deprecated "ghetto" chambers and ten years later, a survey showed that half of all chambers had no ethnic minorities and 53 per cent of non-white barristers were concentrated in 16 sets. The Bar established a Race Relations Committee in 1983 and an equal opportunities policy in 1991. In 2005, the Sutton Trust showed that two thirds of barristers from top chambers were privately educated. In 2007, the Bar published a report by Lord Neuberger, *Entry to the Bar*. He wanted to attract able people from state schools. The Bar introduced a placement programme for state school children to learn about the Bar and the courts. Cherie Booth QC repeatedly complained that commencing at the Bar was too expensive for many students and it was much more difficult to get into practice than it was for a solicitor. In 2011, the Bar Council launched *become-a-barrister.com*, to try to promote social mobility. Nevertheless, by 2013, because the number of new Bar tenancies has been declining every year, Bar entrants have top class degrees.

LEGAL EXECUTIVES AND PARALEGALS

According to the 2012 LSB report, cited below, 40 per cent of fee-earners in firms regulated by the SRA were not solicitors in 2009–10. Much of the everyday work of solicitors' offices is performed by legal executives, paralegals with specialist qualifications. The Chartered Institute of Legal Executives (CILEX) is their representative body for 22,000 legal executives and trainees. They can become partners in a legal disciplinary practice and gain advocacy rights and can now become district judges. The CILEX website provides a description of their work. The CILEX Professional Standards Board is overseen by the LSB.

There are over 250,000–300,000 paralegals in the UK. Some belong to The Institute of Paralegals and some to the National Institute of Licensed Paralegals. Thanks to the abolition of barristers' and solicitors' monopolies since the 1980s and the liberation of legal services by the **LSA 2007**, thousands of legal services firms consist solely of paralegals and this trend may continue.

LEGAL EDUCATION

Legal education and training was reviewed in 2012. Reference should therefore be made to the recommendations and outcomes of this review.

Barristers

All-graduate entry. Non-law graduates and mature students do a one-year Common Professional Examination (CPE) or diploma in law (the academic stage), then they and law graduates take a one-year Bar Professional Training Course (or two years part-time). Students must dine 12 times at their Inn of Court. After this, successful candidates may be called to the Bar. All barristers offering legal services must undertake one year of pupillage and continuing education. The Advocacy Training Council was established in 2011, to help ensure "excellence in advocacy": C. Haddon-Cave QC, *Counsel*, April 2011.

Solicitors

Non-law graduates and mature students do the CPE or diploma in law. Then they and law graduates take the Legal Practice Course (one year, or part-time). This is more flexible from 2009–10. It may be taken in two stages with different providers. Alternatively, students may take a four-year qualifying degree. All must complete a two-year training contract before being admitted. All solicitors must undertake continuing education.

BACKGROUND: THE GRADUAL ABOLITION OF LAWYERS' MONOPOLIES AND RESTRICTIVE PRACTICES

The Solicitors' Conveyancing Monopoly

Solicitors' best-known monopoly was conveyancing. It used to be a substantial fee-earner. The public complained of overcharging. Solicitors claimed the monopoly protected the public from charlatans. The Thatcher Government opposed all monopolies as anti-competitive. A system of licensed conveyancers was introduced by the Administration of Justice Act 1985. In 1989, Lord Mackay L.C. proposed to permit conveyancing by banks and building societies. Solicitors argued that the "unfair competition" from banks and building societies would extinguish most firms of high street solicitors, thus denying the public easy access to legal services. Despite this, he promoted the **CLSA 1990**.

KEY POINT

The statutory objective of the Courts and Legal Services Act 1990 is "making provision for new or better ways of providing such services [advocacy, litigation, probate and conveyancing] and a wider choice of persons providing them, while maintaining the proper and efficient administration of justice" (s.17).

The Act established a board with the general duty to develop competition in conveyancing services and to authorise practitioners. It permitted conveyancing by banks and building societies but this part was so controversial *it was never implemented.*

Repercussions

1. The Law Society permitted solicitors to advertise and worked to identify new markets, for instance, financial services.
2. Conveyancing costs fell.
3. Solicitors began selling houses.

Abolition of the probate and litigation monopolies

The **CLSA 1990** opened up probate services to banks, building societies, insurance companies and legal executives but this restriction was only relaxed *very* slowly. From 2009, barristers and conveyancers were permitted to conduct probate work.

Abolishing the Bar's monopoly over rights of audience

In 1984, retaliating over the threat to its conveyancing monopoly, the Law Society re-launched an attack on the Bar's monopoly over rights of audience in all higher courts. Solicitors have always had a right to argue cases in magistrates' courts and county courts. Barristers enjoyed a customary monopoly, fixed by a committee of judges, over rights of audience in the senior courts. The RCLS 1979 rejected solicitors' arguments on the following grounds.

- If solicitors were permitted rights of audience in the Crown Court, this would destroy the livelihood of junior barristers.
- Jury advocacy involves special skills maintained with practice, which most solicitors could not spare the time to keep up.
- Since it was up to the solicitor to select a barrister, he could make a more informed selection than the client.

In 1986, the two sides established the Marre Committee to stop the battle. They recommended that solicitors should have Crown Court audience rights.

Changes made by the Thatcher Government

Lord Chancellor Mackay was keen to extend the Thatcherite approach to monopolies to the Bar's work. The Government considered that the best public access to legal services was achieved by giving clients the widest choice within a free and efficient market. Amid ferocious opposition by the

Bar and the judges, the proposals were enacted in the **CLSA 1990**. It provided that rights to appear could only be granted by the "appropriate authorised body" and made similar provision for the right to conduct litigation. This allowed the Law Society to authorise solicitors to appear in court.

Repercussions

The threat of competition had an important impact on the Bar. It relaxed a number of its practice rules and even had to acquaint itself with modern business practices.

- Promoting new areas of work and merging chambers.
- Permitting the establishment of chambers outside the Temple.
- Allowing direct access to non-practising, employed barristers by their employers' clients (and ultimately by the public, from 2004).
- Paying pupils and reformed training.

KEY POINT

LIFE AFTER THE COURTS AND LEGAL SERVICES ACT 1990

By 2009, nothing much happened. Licensed conveyancers did not destroy the solicitors' side of the profession because, by 2010, there were under 1,100 of them and over 140,000 solicitors. There have been arguments over rights of audience since the 1970s. The Law Society can now authorise private practitioners as higher court advocates but by 2007 there were about 1,200, many of whom did not use their rights of audience. This was hardly likely to destroy the Bar of over 15,000 and the Bar continued to grow. The big change did not come about until 2009–12. Now, the Crown Prosecution Service uses many employed solicitors and barristers as Crown Court advocates and many independent solicitor-advocates have started to represent defendants in the Crown Court.

A frustrated Labour Lord Chancellor, the Access to Justice Act 1999 and rights of audience

The Labour Lord Chancellor, Lord Irvine, signalled his impatience with the lack of progress made by the **CLSA 1990**, in opening up rights of audience beyond the independent Bar, by promoting the **1999 Act**, which only started to have an impact from about 2009.

- **Section 36** gives all barristers rights of audience in all courts and all solicitors rights of audience and rights to conduct litigation in all courts, subject only to rules prescribed by the Law Society.

- **Section 37** prohibits restrictions on rights of audience for employed lawyers. This was a great victory for the CPS and for employed solicitors. In a consultation paper, Lord Irvine had complained of the "sorry saga" of their six-year attempt to get audience rights. The Bar strongly opposed this on the ground that the interests of justice were better served by an independent advocate.
- **Section 39** makes audience rights portable from one profession to another, if advocates change profession.
- **Section 40** empowers the Bar Council and CILEX as authorised bodies to grant their members rights to conduct litigation.
- **Section 42** imposes on all advocates and litigators a duty to the court and a duty to act in the interests of justice, formerly common law duties.

The Office of Fair Trading continued to attack restrictive practices

Nevertheless, progress had been far too slow, according to the OFT. In its 2001 Report, *Competition in Professions*, it recommended removing unjustified restrictions on competition.

- The QC system should be abolished. They questioned the system as a quality mark, and its value to consumers.
- Multi-disciplinary partnerships of lawyers and others should be permitted.
- The Bar should abolish its prohibition on direct access by most clients. This "requires customers to employ two types of lawyer".
- Advertising should be de-restricted.
- Law Society fee guidance should be abolished as it inhibited price competition.
- Banks and building societies should be permitted to do conveyancing.

The Bar responded by changing its rules, from 2003, to permit barristers of three years' call who have undertaken a special course, to give legal advice, draft documents and act as advocates in certain circumstances without the intervention of a solicitor. See Bar Council website.

The OFT was still critical

In 2002, the OFT insisted that

- the QC system was anti-competitive, lacked quality control and was of little use to customers; and
- the earning power and competitive position of barristers was enhanced but little extra value was offered to clients.

In its 2003 Annual Report, the Commission for Judicial Appointments concluded that the expense of the QC selection procedure was unsustainable:

> "we have built up a picture of wider systemic bias in the way that the judiciary and the legal profession operate that affects the position of women, ethnic minority candidates and solicitors in relation to Silk and judicial appointments".

QC system at last reformed

In 2003, the Labour government published a consultation paper pointing out that no other profession had such a rank. They were recognised only by reputation, not examinations. To solicitors' disappointment, the Lord Chancellor announced that the QC system would stay. Since 2006, selection is made against an agreed set of competences, using self-assessment, multiple references and an interview. Solicitors continue to complain but a commissioned report by Sir Duncan Nicol, in 2009, advised against change.

THE CLEMENTI REPORT ON RESTRUCTURING THE LEGAL PROFESSIONS AND THE LEGAL SERVICES ACT 2007 ("TESCO LAW")

Regulating Lawyers

In 2003, Lord Falconer L.C. announced a review of legal services by Sir David Clementi, to examine what form of regulation would best promote competition, serve consumer interests and be more accountable. He again proposed allowing banks, building societies and insurance companies to handle probate, and permitting supermarkets and other retailers to provide legal services (thus implementing the **CLSA 1990**), and allowing law firms to use outside investment. The **Legal Services Act 2007** had a rough passage through Parliament, as a bill, and provoked media controversy. One serious concern was the creation of the Legal Services Board, as a government-funded super-regulator, with statutory powers over the professional regulatory bodies. Opponents and foreign bars were concerned about maintaining the profession's independence, drawing attention to the UN Basic Principles on the Role of Lawyers, requiring public access to independent lawyers.

KEY POINT

Clementi reported in *Review of the Regulatory Framework for Legal Services in England and Wales* (2004), favouring "a regulatory framework which permits a high degree of choice" for consumer and lawyer.

- He recommended that legal disciplinary practices (LDPs) should be considered. These are now permitted by the **LSA 2007**, since March 2009. Any lawyers can be allowed to practise together. For instance, legal executives can now become partners; solicitors can be managers of a firm of licensed conveyancers and a firm of solicitors can be joined by patent and trade mark attorneys. Managers can include non-lawyers; 75 per cent must be lawyers. LDPs can take the form of partnerships, companies or LLPs—limited liability partnerships. Individual lawyers will be regulated by their own professions. A solicitors' firm can now combine with a set of barristers' chambers, subject to Bar Standards Board rules.
- Clementi also recommended reconsidering multi-disciplinary partnerships. These had been considered since the 1970s. In an MDP, solicitors could be partners with other business people, such as estate agents and accountants. The Act permits these "alternative business structures" since 2011.
- Barristers may join alternative business structures. They may form barrister-only partnerships. They may even apply to conduct litigation.
- Clementi recommended that investment in LDPs could come from outside owners (e.g. Tesco) but they would need to be "fit to own", and there should be no conflict of interest. An insurance company could not own, say, a personal injury firm.

IMPACT OF THE LSA 2007 ON LAWYERS' BUSINESS STRUCTURES AND THE RISE OF THE PARALEGAL LAW FIRM

Newspapers and law journals have been full of speculation about the potential impact on lawyers' business structures. Ironically, Tesco displayed no interest but the Co-op set up legal services outlets from 2011 and is now an ABS. It launched its family department in 2012, offering fixed fees and "jargon free" services. (N.L.J. news, 21 September). According to Legal Risk, only five per cent of the top 100 law firms believe the Act will have "a significant" impact on them. C. McConnell considers that firms that practice internationally are not likely to transform into ABS or accept outside ownership because both are banned by the American Bar Association and there are similar problems in Europe. High Street firms will be affected because supermarkets and others will sell commoditised, standardised legal products: (2009) 159 N.L.J. 1069. Typifying this prediction, LegalZoom and QualitySolicitors are launching online documents in 2012, relating to employment, divorce, wills and company formations. A 2009 survey by Intendance Research found almost half of lawyers surveyed thought high street firms would be drastically affected. The **2007 Act** regulates reserved legal services, which include rights of audience, litigation, probate and so on but in 2010, Professor Stephen Mayson found that 80 percent of what most firms do was unreserved work: legal advice; tribunal work; will writing; and negotiation. Therefore, a law firm could confine itself to these legal services and avoid regulation.

Irrespective of the **LSA 2007**, small law firms have been "quietly facing tough competition from non-solicitor, i.e. paralegal, law firms (PLFs) for years now", according to James O'Connell, solicitor and CEO of the Institute of Paralegals. He drew attention to the 6,500 paralegal firms that had developed over the previous 15 years. As he said, some small firms of lawyers would be better off removing themselves from the roll of solicitors to escape the burden of their insurance premiums. He argued that paralegal firms were more innovative in finding new areas of work and providing services of the type and in a manner that suits potential clients: (2011) 161 N.L.J. 1453.

Over the last 20 years, solicitors have lost some personal injury work to claims management companies, who aggressively advertise their services to accident victims. They grew 184 per cent in 2006–11, according to the LSB report, below. Some PI firms have, however, benefited from these companies because they have had cases referred to them. In exchange, solicitors paid a fee for these referrals. Referral fees have now been banned by the **Legal Aid, Sentencing and Punishment of Offenders Act 2012**.

By July 2012, eight firms had been licensed by the Solicitors Regulation Authority as ABSs, including a non-solicitor firm. One is foreign-owned and is part of a company listed on the Stock Exchange. Some firms looking for outside investors, in order to become an ABS, will struggle because of the recession. A 2012 survey of 100 commercial law firms by Jures found that about about 40 per cent had changed their management strategy as a result of the **2007 Act**. Most respondents cited access to private equity finance as a compelling reason to convert to an ABS. In August, Irwin Mitchell became the largest firm to become an ABS. In the meantime, barristers realised they needed to re-think their business practices in order to compete. Some barristers are setting up firms to provide legal advice direct to consumers for a fixed fee. Also, an organisation called Riverview has linked 75 lawyers, 43 of whom are barristers, including 12 QCs. They offer advice contracts to corporate clients. See J. Robins at (2012) 162 N.L.J. 887 and 1103. A group of barristers' chambers has created *barristerlink.com*, allowing solicitors to check barrister availability.

CLEMENTI AND THE LSA 2007 ON COMPLAINTS

The RCLS 1979 condemned the Law Society's handling of complaints and, despite reform, it had been criticised ever since. In the **Access to Justice Act 1999**, the Lord Chancellor was empowered to appoint a Legal Services Commissioner if the Law Society did not correct the problem. In 2000, the Director General of Fair Trading gave the Law Society a "final warning" to put their house in order. Very controversially, Clementi suggested abolishing the legal profession's right to self-regulation. All complaints would be made to an independent Office for Legal Complaints (OLC). Its aim would be to provide "quick and fair redress to consumers", including mediation and making binding orders. These proposals were enacted in the **2007 Act**. It was heavily criticised by lawyers and had to be amended. In 2012, according to LSB research, over 80 per cent of clients are satisfied with the services provided by solicitors and other lawyers.

FUSION

It has long been argued that the public would be better served by a fused profession, instead of the traditional division of labour, with the solicitor seeing the client, then briefing the barrister, who appears in court. The abolition of lawyers' monopolies and restrictive practices is resulting in a significant blurring of the line. There are already 62 mixed solicitor-barrister practices providing advocacy services. (J. Wotton (2012) LS Gaz, 2 Feb). Many barristers fear that this will result in the death of the bar. Wotton thinks that competition from solicitor advocates will result in barristers concentrating on "the senior end of the spectrum".

Arguments for fusion

- If a case goes to court, unless it is argued by a solicitor-advocate, the client is often paying for two lawyers, a barrister and solicitor, or three if a QC is employed ("three taxi meters", as Zander famously said, in *Lawyers and the Public Interest*, 1968).
- Because the client tells the story to the solicitor, then the solicitor briefs the barrister, there may be a failure in communication and the system is inefficient.
- Returned briefs: clients and solicitors are frequently denied their first

choice of barrister, because she is unavailable, so the brief is passed to someone else in the same chambers.

Arguments against

- Barristers can concentrate on preparing for trial, or preparing a specialist opinion, free from interruptions to meet clients.
- Jury advocacy and oral advocacy are specialist skills which need constant development.
- Loss of choice: if the profession were fused, the best barristers would join law firms and cease to be available to all clients.
- The present system is more cost effective. It is cheaper to brief a barrister as an advocate because solicitors' practices have a lot of overheads.
- English procedure requires continuous hearings and solicitors cannot spare the time for this.
- Judges are not expected to research cases so they depend on the specialist legal knowledge of barristers.

Revision Checklist

You should now know and understand the following:

- **the statistical distribution of barristers and solicitors and issues of diversity;**
- **the destruction of lawyers' monopolies and restrictive practices and the reasoning behind this (to open up competition);**
- **the structure, education and organisation of the legal profession;**
- **the new regulatory structure established by the LSA 2007; and**
- **new business structures permitted by the LSA 2007 and likely impact.**

FURTHER READING/UPDATING

Darbyshire on the ELS, 2011, Chapter 13
New Law Journal
The Law Society's *Gazette*

websites

Bar Council
CILEX
Law Society
Regulatory bodies, as mentioned in the text

QUESTION AND ANSWER

The Question

Explain and account for the dismantling of the monopolies and restrictive practices that separated the two sides of the legal profession and marked them out from other lawyers such as legal executives. Would a fused profession better serve the public interest?

Advice and the answer

Advice

"Explain and account for" means tell the story of events and explain the reasons why it happened. There are two parts to the question and they are not divided into a. and b. so they may well be related. Indeed, here they are related. If all monopolies and restrictive practices are abolished then any lawyer can do anything, even if they have to acquire special qualifications, so this would ultimately lead to a fused profession, something the Bar have long feared as threatening its survival as a separate profession.

Answer guide

1. Examine the whittling away of barristers' rights of audience, solicitors' conveyancing monopoly, solicitors' monopoly over direct access to the client and their monopoly over probate services. Examine changes to the QC system.
2. It does not matter whether you tell the story about monopolies in chronological order or describe what happened to the monopolies one by one, provided that there is a clear plan and you demonstrate an understanding of how the issues are related.
3. In this part of your answer, there is no need to refer to lawyers' regulatory structure.
4. Explain that this anti-monopoly policy was meant to open up competition and thus enhance consumer interests.
5. Comment on what has been achieved for the profession and the consumer.
6. Note that it has taken a long time and several Lord Chancellors to partly dismantle these monopolies and
7. We are still only part way there, because solicitors still strongly object to the QC system and continue to call for its abolition.

8. Consider the pros and cons of a unified profession.
9. Acknowledge the Bar's fear that dismantling monopolies then establishing new business structures open to all types of lawyer, under the **LSA 2007**, may result in a fused profession and destroy the independent Bar.
10. Though they have been expressing this fear since the 1970s, the Bar is still thriving. Indeed, examining the statistics, both sides continue to grow year on year BUT, by 2013, we are beginning to see the effects of the abolition of monopolies with large numbers of solicitor advocates and employed lawyers now appearing in the Crown Court, and growth of the Bar almost stagnating.
11. You might add a comment that whether or not the two main elements of the legal profession fuse, more legal services are being provided by the 6,500 paralegal firms, which far outnumber solicitors and barristers put together.
12. Reach a brief conclusion, summarising what you have said.

Judges

8

INTRODUCTION

This chapter examines judicial independence, then how judges are selected, appointed, trained, disciplined and removed. It examines the controversy surrounding selection and composition and the slow road to reform, culminating in the **Constitutional Reform Act 2005**.

KEY POINT

Since the 1950s, the most controversial point has been judges' narrow social and educational background. Around 75 per cent of *senior* judges were independently schooled, the majority being Oxbridge graduates and almost all appointed from the senior (QC) rank of the Bar. Minorities and women are underrepresented. The narrowness of the judiciary was partly attributable to the old-boy network selection system, based on "consultations" with existing judges, which was not fully removed until 2006, by the **2005 Act**. The Act dismantled the tripartite role of the Lord Chancellor (L.C.), with important jobs in all three organs of government and thus an obvious breach of the separation of powers.

TYPES OF JUDGE

The court structure diagram indicates the courts in which the different ranks sit. Some, such as tribunal judges, are not described here but all types are described on the Judiciary website, which also contains current diversity statistics. Most criminal cases are heard by lay magistrates, described in the next chapter.

- Recorders are lawyers who sit at least 15 days per year in the Crown and/or county court. Part-time sitting is normally a requirement for a fulltime post.
- District judges (DJs) in the county court manage and hear *most* civil and family cases. Each has sat as a part-time deputy before applying.

- District judges (magistrates' courts) (DJMCs) hear mainly criminal cases but also civil and family. They have an identical jurisdiction to lay magistrates, except some are authorised to hear extradition cases and they tend to be used for longer and more complex cases. Like magistrates, they are arbiters of fact and law so they are very powerful. In criminal cases, they determine the verdict (guilt or innocence), decide points of law and do the sentencing. Each has sat as a deputy.
- Circuit judges (CJs) hear most Crown Court cases and many sit only in the Crown Court. In trials, they sit with a jury whose job it is to bring in the verdict, so the judge determines points of law, conducts the trial, determines the admissibility of evidence and does the sentencing. Some also sit, or sit exclusively, in the county court, hearing the more complex civil and family cases. Most HC cases outside London are heard by authorised ("ticketed") CJs. In rare civil jury trials, they conduct the trial and determine the points of law. The jury determines liability and damages. A very small number are authorised to sit in the Court of Appeal (Criminal Division) (CACD).
- District judges of the HC sit in the Principal Registry of the Family Division. Their work is similar to a family CJ.
- HC Masters manage most HC cases in London.
- HC judges mostly sit in the Queen's Bench Division (QBD). Judges in the Chancery and Family Divisions are recruited from specialist lawyers. Most divide their time between London and the circuits. Most appeals in the CACD are heard by QBD judges, chaired by a Lord Justice of Appeal. HC judges sit occasionally in the CA (Civil Division).
- Lords Justices of Appeal (L.J.s) mostly sit in both Divisions of the CA, determining appeals on points of law and fact, and appeals against sentence. They also sit in the Divisional Court of the QBD. Many have management jobs, organising the CA and HC and supervising the rest of the judiciary. They are recruited from the HC.
- UK Supreme Court (UKSC) Justices hear points of law of general public importance, from all over the UK, and also sit in the Judicial Committee of the Privy Council (JCPC), mainly determining appeals from the Commonwealth. There is normally one from N. Ireland and two from Scotland. The others are usually recruited from the CA but Lord Sumption was recruited direct from the Bar. They are styled "Lord" or "Lady" for life, as a courtesy title, but are not members of the House of Lords.

THE HEADS OF DIVISION

The Lord Chief Justice

As a result of the **2005 Act**, he replaced the Lord Chancellor (L.C.) as head of the judiciary in 2006. He represents judges' views to Government and Parliament. He is responsible for the welfare, training and guidance of the judiciary, and for judicial deployment. He is President of the Courts. He chairs the Judges' Council and Sentencing Council. If the **Crime and Courts Bill** is enacted, he will replace the L.C. in appointing judges below the High Court. Since 2006, he is appointed by a specially convened panel of the Judicial Appointments Commission.

The Master of the Rolls

The M.R. is the President of the CA (Civil Division) and Head of Civil Justice.

The President of the QBD

This post was created by the **2005 Act**. He is also Head of Criminal Justice.

The President of the Family Division

He heads the Family Division of the HC and is Head of Family Justice.

The Chancellor of the High Court

This post, formerly Vice Chancellor, was renamed in the **2005 Act**. He heads the Chancery Division.

INDEPENDENCE

It is a fundamental constitutional requirement that judges are independent, that is, beyond the influence of the executive government, apolitical, incorruptible and unbiased. Independence is also required as a UN basic principle and by art.6 of the **European Convention**. Rules and conventions support this and are bolstered by s.3 of the **2005 Act**, which places a duty on all ministers and those involved in the administration of justice to uphold judicial independence.

1. Security of tenure: under the **Act of Settlement 1700**, senior judges may only be removed by both Houses of Parliament.
2. Salaries: are fixed by a non-governmental body.
3. Apolitical: judges are statute-barred from being M.P.s. and traditionally do not engage in party political debates. Historically, the office of L.C. fell foul of this rule and of art.6 of the **ECHR**, because he held important

positions in all three organs of government. He was speaker of the House of Lords (legislature), a very powerful cabinet member (executive) and was head of the judiciary and entitled to sit as a judge, chairing the law lords. In 2003, the Government announced that his position was untenable. Under the **CRA 2005**, he ceased to be head of the judiciary and he lost his former power to appoint or select most judges. Selection is now done by the Judicial Appointments Commission and appointment is by the Queen. The L.C. remains in the Cabinet as the minister in charge of courts and legal services. In 2003, the Government also announced that the law lords breached the separation of powers, being peers in the House of Lords as well as the UK's most important judges. The **CRA 2005** replaced them with a UK Supreme Court, in 2009.

4. Judges cannot be sued for remarks in court.
5. Parliamentarians should not criticise judges.
6. Politicians should refrain from criticising judges. This convention seemed to be forgotten by several Labour ministers.
7. The media should refrain from criticising judges: this convention seems to have fallen into disuse. Judges suffer from a negative media image: see Darbyshire, *Sitting in Judgment* (2011), Ch.2.
8. Freedom from interference with decision making.
9. The rule against bias: judges are disqualified by common law (the rules of natural justice), from dealing with cases in which they have an interest, proprietary or personal. This is now reiterated in art.6 of the **ECHR**. See *Belize Bank v AG of Belize* [2011] UKPC 36, discussed by M. Elliott, at (2012) 71(2) C.L.J. 247, on *Westlaw*.
10. Appointments: the system must be independent. In 2011–12, the House of Lords, in its inquiry, mentioned below, asked whether Parliament should scrutinise the appointment process, but the British have always been very hostile to this prospect, reminiscent of the sometimes undignified and always politicised public appointment hearings of US Supreme Court nominees.
11. Regular use is made of judicial independence by appointing them to head inquiries into politically sensitive issues.

In 2007, the Labour government was criticised by the House of Lords Constitutional Affairs Committee because they created a Ministry of Justice without consulting the judges and did not seem to understand the constitutional implications of this. Senior judges were concerned about judicial independence and safeguarding the courts budget.

NEUTRALITY

Writers such as J.A.G. Griffith in *The Politics of The Judiciary* (1977) were, however, less concerned over the previously-declared political allegiance of the judiciary than over their narrow political and social class backgrounds and socialisation at the Bar, consciously or unconsciously influencing them, especially in political cases (e.g. labour relations, civil liberties, students and immigrants, etc.). Griffith and other critics argued, in the 1960s and 1970s, that judges showed a significantly "right-wing" approach. This criticism could not be applied to modern judges, viewed by governments as a liberal nuisance, promoting human rights. Senior judges still come from narrow social and educational backgrounds and there are too few women and minorities. I have called the composition of the judiciary an international embarrassment. Nevertheless, in *Sitting in Judgment*, I pointed out that criticism of the senior judiciary as over-representing Oxbridge is silly. In all judiciaries, worldwide, top judges come from the top universities. They have to analyse massive amounts of very complex data. We ought to be concerned if they had *not* been educated to the highest level. The fact that Oxbridge has a class-biased intake is a separate problem.

QUALIFICATIONS

The Courts and Legal Services Act 1990 reformed eligibility for appointment by basing it on rights of audience (rights to appear in court). Solicitors had been eligible up to the circuit bench and barristers eligible for all appointments. This had been a source of controversy between the two sides of the profession, solicitors arguing that making them eligible for the HC would widen the pool of candidates, thus diversifying the judiciary. Whilst the **CLSA 1990** made solicitors with rights of audience eligible, there was only one solicitor among 162 senior judges, as of 2012. The Act was criticised by the pressure group JUSTICE, in *The Judiciary in England and Wales* (1992). Practice as an advocate, they argued, did not guarantee the qualities necessary for a good judge. As part of the current attempt to diversify the judiciary, the **Tribunals, Courts and Enforcement Act 2007** amended the qualifications for judicial posts. Instead of requiring audience rights (advocacy rights), or service as a lower-ranking judge, applicants must satisfy an "eligibility condition", meaning account may be taken of their experience as a paralegal or academic, or patent or trade-mark agent. It permits the L.C. to extend qualification to legal executives and members of other designated bodies.

NEW APPOINTMENTS SYSTEM FROM 2006

The Judicial Appointments Commission (JAC), created by the **CRA 2005**, selects judicial office holders. The 15 Commissioners comprise lawyers, judges, magistrates, tribunal members and members of the public. Selection has been radically reformed. All judicial posts must be applied for through competitions. The selection process is tailored to each competition. Candidates complete a lengthy application and provide referees. They sit written tests, set by judges, which are a tool for short-listing. These are designed to assess legal reasoning, forensic judgment and the ability to make and explain decisions. Candidates may be asked to attend an assessment day and will go before an interview panel. See JAC website and J. Sumption, *Counsel*, April 2011.

The first members of the UKSC were mostly the existing law lords. Each time a Justice is needed, a Selection Commission is appointed, consisting of the President and Deputy President of the SC and one member from the JACs of Scotland, Northern Ireland and England and Wales. The selected candidate's name must be passed to the L.C. for recommendation for appointment by the Queen and he can only ask the Commission to reconsider in limited circumstances. "Acting judges", such as retired S.C. Justices, may supplement the S.C. Justices. The background is contained in a 2003 Department of Constitutional Affairs consultation paper, *Constitutional Reform: a Supreme Court for the UK*.

When a new L.C.J. or Head of Division is needed, a special selection panel is convened, consisting of two lay members of the JAC and two senior judges. As for other judges, when there is a vacancy, the JAC will select one candidate. That name is put forward to the L.C. and he may only reject or ask for reconsideration once, in very limited circumstances, otherwise he must appoint that person or put that name forward for appointment by the Queen. For Lord Justices (members of the CA) and above, the L.C. formally recommends the candidate to the Prime Minister for appointment by the Queen.

KEY POINT

The **2005 Act** requires the JAC to encourage diversity and specifies that "selection must be solely on merit" and that appointees must be of good character. The LC may issue guidance but the procedure is for them to determine. This is the first time that selection criteria have been set out in statute.

From 2006, the Judicial Appointments and Conduct Ombudsman investigates complaints about judicial appointment and ensures that complaints about judicial conduct are properly handled.

Background: Progressive reform

Under the pre-2006 system, the L.C. selected all judges, except that the most senior judges were selected by him and the Prime Minister. Considering that the L.C.'s role was a blatant breach of the separation of powers, it placed him in a very powerful position. This led to accusations of party political bias and cronyism. The appointments system had been criticised in the 1970s by Griffith, the pressure group JUSTICE and others, and was progressively reformed from the 1980s, as described here, but this did not deal with the fundamental problem that selection was effectively made by a single man, the L.C., who occupied a controversially powerful role. Traditionally, all judges were selected by the "tap on the shoulder" method—invited to join the bench. For evocative stories of how judges were selected see Darbyshire, *Sitting in Judgment* (2011).

1960s and 70s

In 1968, Abel-Smith and Stevens, then a 1972 JUSTICE subcommittee, considered that a more formal system of applications and references was inevitable. They suggested an advisory committee of lawyers, judges and laymen. By the 1970s, all posts lower than HC had to be applied for.

Lord Hailsham's Era

In 1985, Lord Hailsham described his method of selecting judges and it remained in place with little change until after 2000. He applied three principles:

- to appoint solely on merit;
- no single person's view on a candidate should be regarded as decisive; and
- candidates should not be appointed until they had proven themselves in a part-time capacity.

Senior civil servants gathered factual information from the candidate and opinions from the judiciary and senior members of the profession, who knew the candidate, in "consultations". These were kept on file, the factual information being open to the candidate's inspection.

Lord Mackay's Era

The Law Society argued that this system, with its reliance on advocacy experience and existing judges' personal recommendations, discriminated against women, ethnic minorities and solicitors, regardless of the L.C.'s assurances that he was keen to recruit judges from these groups. In 1996-97 the Association of Women Barristers criticised the appointments system as being biased against women. In 1999, the Law Society announced a boycott of the consultation process, which they called "secret soundings". Groups such as JUSTICE repeatedly criticised the system as based on the say-so of one person, a member of the government. This was an anachronism stemming from the days when the L.C. knew all the candidates. In 1992, they suggested a Judicial Appointments Commission. Lord Mackay L.C. resisted this suggestion but in 1993 he announced a programme of reform, introducing competitions below HC level. A more structured basis for consultations with the judiciary was devised. Lay people were involved as advisers.

Lord Irvine's Era

In 1997, New Labour came to power and announced plans for a Judicial Appointment Commission but Lord Irvine L.C. curiously retracted from them. In 1999, he asked Sir Leonard Peach to review the appointments process. The L.C. revealed that potential judges were continuously assessed by lawyers and judges for such qualities as humanity, courtesy and understanding of society. Peach's evaluation was favourable but he was not allowed to comment on who should make appointments. He recommended the creation of an appointments commission, purely to audit the process. Advocacy should no longer be an essential element. Irvine accepted that. Peach proposed alternative selection methods, such as one-day assessment centres and psychometric testing. He thought more judges should be promoted from the lower ranks. The Law Society called the system an "old boy" network and demanded an end to "secret soundings". In 2000, it published *Broadening the Bench*, outlining proposals for reform. Lord Irvine responded by making continuous reforms to the system but would not contemplate creating an appointing commission, or reforming his office, that of Lord Chancellor, to deal with its breach of separation of powers. He accepted the need for wider advertising, better aptitude testing and an easier route from other judicial roles. A report by Malleson and Banda, *Factors Affecting the Decision to Apply for Silk and Judicial Office* had exposed widespread dissatisfaction with the selection process, especially among women, solicitors and minorities, who felt disadvantaged by the consultations process and resented recruitment from the apparent elite group of barristers' chambers. Many others called for a proper appointments commission, including Lord Steyn (law lord) and the Society of Labour Lawyers.

Judicial performance appraisal was extended from tribunals to the lay magistracy, then to deputy DJs in the late 1990s and to all part-time appointments from 2001. Upper and lower age-limits for most judicial appointments were removed in an attempt to encourage more applications from women and minority lawyers. From 1998, HC posts were advertised and applications invited, though the L.C. reserved the right to invite lawyers to join the HC bench.

Assessment centres were piloted in 2002–03 for deputy DJs and masters of the HC, instead of traditional interviews. The assessments include practical exercises and role-play, an interview and written examination. In 2003, they were reported to be a success and were extended to recorder recruitment. In 2002, a working party recommended making CPS lawyers eligible for appointment, in order to widen social composition. The CPS employs a higher percentage of ethnic minority, female and state-educated lawyers than the legal profession and judiciary as a whole.

The Judicial Appointments Annual Report 2001–02 showed that the percentage of women appointed to judicial posts increased to 34.4 per cent. The proportion of ethnic minority appointments increased to 7.8 per cent. Nevertheless, the pressure for reform became irresistible by 2003. Sir Colin Campbell, First Commissioner for Judicial Appointments, suggested that although the system overall produced excellent judges, it lacked transparency and fairness. The CJA Annual Report 2003 criticised the system as systemically biased against women, ethnic minorities and solicitors. It rejected the notion of a "trickle up" of women and minorities. The consultation process produced too little information to justify its cost and yielded some "narrow and inappropriate views". Also in 2003, Lady Hale became the first woman to be appointed as a Lord of Appeal (now a UKSC Justice). She is heavily critical of the gender imbalance in the judiciary. Crucially, in 2003, a parliamentary select committee scrutinising the L.C.'s Department received witness evidence that the L.C.'s role, breaching the separation of powers, flouted the **ECHR**. At the same time, critics, notably law lords Lords Steyn and Bingham, reiterated the call to separate the law lords from Parliament, as a Supreme Court.

Lord Falconer's Era

The Government, surprisingly, responded to all this by announcing in 2003 that the L.C.'s roles were to be broken up. Lord Irvine L.C. was replaced by Charlie Falconer, in the new post of Secretary of State for Constitutional Affairs and, supposedly, the last L.C. The Government published a set of consultation papers on constitutional reform: on the QC system, the L.C., the Supreme Court and judicial appointments. Papers and responses are on the archived Department of Constitutional Affairs (DCA) website. The paper on judicial appointments suggested three alternative types of JAC: an appointing commission, a recommending commission or a hybrid commission. The Government settled for the second, and this was created in the **2005 Act**, with procedure as described above.

Post-2006: the continuing aim to diversify the judiciary

Apart from the fact that the judiciary is predominantly white and male (diversity statistics are on the judiciary's website), much research and comment has been devoted to their narrow social background. Griffith demonstrated that at least 75 per cent of most judicial samples surveyed came from upper or upper-middle class families, and attended public school and then Oxford or Cambridge. See now statistics published by the Sutton Trust. Lord Falconer L.C. considered lack of diversity to be an urgent problem. In 2004, he published a consultation paper, *Increasing Diversity in the Judiciary*, saying: "Society must have confidence in that the judiciary has a real understanding of the problems facing people from all sectors of society". The paper and responses are on the archived DCA website. In 2006, the DCA published a *Judicial Diversity Strategy*. It resulted from research on what deters women and minorities from applying. During and since Lord Mackay's era, the 1980s, big efforts have been made to recruit a more representative pool of candidates. Fractional posts and job-shares have been put in place. Judges often give lectures on diversity. See also the **Tribunals, Courts and Enforcement Act 2007**, above.

Remember that the Judicial Appointments Commission has a statutory duty to promote diversity under the **2005 Act**. It has a JAC Diversity Forum, whose work is explained in the JAC *Annual Report*. Its first chair, Baroness Prashar, said that if the judiciary was to diversify, the legal profession needed to make itself more diverse. In 2008, the JAC commissioned independent research to find out what attracts people to, or puts them off, applying to the senior judiciary, surveying 6000 members of the judiciary. These reports indicated that the following factors discourage potential applicants and these are outside the control of the JAC:

- the policy of requiring applicants to have served part-time (in fee paid work);
- lack of availability of *salaried* fractional full-time appointments;
- a lack of diversity among lawyers; and
- working conditions within the judiciary. (2008–09 Annual Report.)

Professor Dame Hazel Genn's report for the Judicial Executive Board on the attractiveness of senior judicial appointment, published in 2009, also helped identify why some lawyers are deterred from applying for high judicial office. (See Judiciary website news release 01/09.) The numbers of solicitors applying for judicial appointments remains low. Solicitors make up about 90 per cent of eligible appointees and are from a more diverse background than barristers. The JAC research in 2009 showed that "unfounded myths" were deterring applicants. The proportion of women in the senior judiciary, 22 of 161 in 2012, remains a strikingly low number, though they are disproportionately successful in competitions at the lowest level. For instance, in 2011–12, they took 43 per cent of DJ places, though they comprised only 19 per cent of applicants.

Baroness Neuberger headed a committee which resulted in *The Report of the Advisory Panel on Judicial Diversity*, 2010. Its main conclusions were as follows.

- The judiciary should reflect the diversity of society and the legal profession, to enhance public confidence.
- We lack a coherent strategy. We need to address everything from the legal career to judicial retention and promotion.
- The JAC should emphasise its commitment to diversity.
- Heads of the legal profession need to be included in the effort.

A judicial diversity task force was established and in September 2012 they published a progress report, claiming to have achieved 20 of Lady Neuberger's 53 goals. By 2011–12 we have reached an almost obsessional phase of asking whether more could be done to diversify the judiciary, yet the legal profession itself is insufficiently diverse, as we saw in the last chapter, and no amount of efforts seem to have persuaded enough solicitors and women to apply for judicial appointments. In the 2012 competition for circuit judge, heavyweight crime, only 18 of the 126 applicants were women. The Law Society has launched yet another drive to persuade solicitors to apply in 2012. In 2011, the House of Lords constitution committee launched an inquiry into the appointments process, reporting in March 2012 (see Parliament website). There is nothing new in their recommendations, except that they support the application of the Equalities Act 2010, meaning that if two candidates of equal merit are appointable, the minority candidate wins. This supports the MoJ's 2011 report on its consultation, *A Judiciary for the 21st Century*. It also proposed that some of the L.C.'s powers should be transferred to the L.C.J., and an independent lay person should chair the selection panels for the L.C.J. and the President of the UKSC. These changes are contained in the **Crime and Courts Bill 2012**. In May 2012, the Government announced that there would be more salaried part-time judges and a greater lay involvement in appointing judges. There are over 70 diversity and community relations judges doing outreach work and mentoring students from low income backgrounds as part of the Social Mobility Foundation programme. See data analysis by M. Blackwell, at [2012] P.L. 426.

PROMOTION

There is no career judiciary. A circuit judge does not expect to be "promoted" to the HC. Most circuit and HC judges are recruited from the legal profession, not from the ranks of district judges. Career judiciaries are a common pattern elsewhere in Europe, where law graduates may choose to train for the judiciary rather than practise, and can expect promotion in the same manner as the civil service. Their judges are consequently much younger than ours. In 1992, JUSTICE repeated its 1972 suggestion of a structured judicial career path and the Labour Government sought views on a career judiciary in its 2003 consultation paper.

TRAINING

They receive very little, compared with European career judges, who have proper colleges. The Judicial College, formerly Studies Board, is a virtual college, supervises brief initial training for new part-time judges in the lower judiciary, and all the lower judiciary receive regular continuation training. New HC judges received no special training until 2003 and the senior judiciary are not provided with systematic continuation training or expected to attend, though from 2009, induction training for HC judges has been devised with each head of division, comprising sitting-in and visits. From 2011–12, seminars in civil and family cases have been offered. CA judges chair specialist sessions for HC and CA judges. All judges have access to online materials. Specialist sessions for the whole judiciary have been run on major reforms such as the **Civil Procedure Rules 1998** and **Human Rights Act 1998**. Judges resisted training until the 1970s on the ground that it undermined independence. Consequently, the College is run by judges and most training is delivered by judges.

REMOVAL

It is a corollary of judicial independence and immunity that judges, especially the senior judiciary, have an entrenched security of tenure, first established in the **Act of Settlement 1700**. Now, under the Supreme Court Act 1981 (**Senior Courts Act**) and the **CRA 2005** every senior judge "shall hold office during good behaviour, subject to a power of removal by Her Majesty, on an address presented to her by both Houses of Parliament". This procedure has only been used once to remove an Irish Admiralty judge in 1830 for embezzlement. The L.C. may remove an infirm judge, incapacitated from resigning, under the **Senior Courts Act** s.11. Under the **Courts Act 1971** s.17, he may remove a circuit judge on the grounds of incapacity or misbehaviour, or failure to comply with his conditions of appointment. Judge Bruce Campbell was so removed in 1983 after his well-publicised convictions for smuggling large quantities of whisky and cigarettes. Under the **CRA 2005**, removal now needs the L.C.J.'s consent and a recommendation from a special tribunal but most judges resign before this might arise, such as a circuit judge convicted for drink-driving in 2009. See further Darbyshire, *Sitting in Judgment.*

COMPLAINTS

Under the **CRA 2005**, the L.C. and L.C.J. have joint responsibility for complaints and discipline of judges and magistrates, and are assisted by the Office for Judicial Complaints. Previously, there was no formal system.

RESEARCH

The UCL Judicial Studies Institute was launched in 2010. Until now, there has been little or no research on judges' work, except books on the law lords, notably Paterson's brilliant 1970s study. My 2011 book, *Sitting in Judgment*, reports eight years of in-depth observation of judges at work. I work-shadowed 40 judges, from DJs up to UKSC Justices, in civil cases, family and crime, in a broad spread of their work, talking to them and observing them all day. I interviewed 77 judges and met many more. This work is unique, world-wide, in its breadth and depth. I asked the judges about their careers, what prompted them to apply to be judges or what it was like to be "tapped on the shoulder", what they thought of their training, whether being a judge changed them, what they thought of their work, and what worried them. I found that most judges did not come from legal families. They were inspired by TV programmes as children. Because all human life and frailty is paraded before them, they are far more *in touch* with the real world than the journalists who try and portray them as fogeys. A number came from underprivileged backgrounds. HC and CA judges and some senior CJs work extremely long hours.

Revision Checklist

You should now know and understand:

- **the main types of judge, including Heads of Division, the courts they sit in and the work they do;**
- **the eleven aspects of judicial independence;**
- **what is meant by judicial neutrality;**
- **how judges are recruited, selected, trained, disciplined and removed;**
- **the importance of the CRA 2005 in reforming the judicial appointment system and the role of L.C.;**
- **the background of complaints and reform that preceded the 2005 Act; and**
- **the problem of lack of diversity and the attempts to enhance diversity.**

FURTHER READING/UPDATING

Darbyshire on the ELS, 2011, Chapter 14 and material referred to therein, and updates on the Sweet & Maxwell website.

P. Darbyshire, *Sitting in Judgment – the working lives of judges* (2011)

Websites

Department of Constitutional Affairs (archived)

Judiciary

Judicial Appointments Commission, especially annual report and publications

Judicial College, annual reports and prospectuses

Office for Judicial Complaints

QUESTION AND ANSWER

The Question

Explain how and why the system of judicial appointments has recently been reformed. In your opinion, is there room for further improvement in recruiting and selecting judges?

Advice and the Answer

The reforms are explained in this book and in greater detail in *Darbyshire on the ELS*, 2011. The best sources for prompting you to think about how the system could be further reformed are the consultation papers on judicial appointments 2003 and judicial diversity, 2004, as above, and responses, archived on the DCA website. You may think, for instance, that the law should be changed so that judicial appointments are not confined to lawyers with relevant rights of audience or that the post-qualification periods stipulated in the law should be reduced. You might consider whether academics should be eligible for appointment as judges but if you make any suggestions, ensure that you justify them.

1. Explain the traditional and current criticism of the judiciary, that it (especially the senior judiciary) is dominated by older, white males, a disproportionate number of whom were independently schooled and Oxbridge educated. See stats on diversity on the Judiciary website. Find Sutton Trust stats on educational background.
2. Explain how this was/is partly caused by the old system of recruitment, pre-2006, with its heavy reliance on existing judges' views (hardly surprising that judges recommended people like themselves).
3. Explain how it was partly caused by the historic statutory requirement for judges to be selected from barristers and solicitors with rights of audience, thus narrowing the pool significantly.
4. Describe the progressive pre-2006 reforms and the new scheme under the **CRA 2005** and the change of statutory qualifications for the bench in the **2007 Act** and show how they were intended to respond to previous criticisms and make the recruitment system fairer and open to a wider pool. Comment.
5. Acknowledge the new complaint that judges are still not being

recruited from a diverse pool and the JAC's response that this is caused by lack of diversity in the legal profession itself. Cross check information in the previous chapter of this book on the legal profession. See JAC website, annual reports and the research mentioned above.

6. Consider the 2004 paper on diversity and all of the many research papers on the JAC website, the Neuberger report and the recent Ministry of Justice consultations.
7. Think about and suggest further reforms that might help to diversify the judiciary and acknowledge any hurdles.
8. Make brief concluding remarks, summarizing what you have said.

Magistrates

INTRODUCTION

This chapter covers magistrates, who sit in the magistrates' court, hearing and sentencing the bulk of criminal cases and many family cases and hearing appeals in the Crown Court, and district judges' (magistrates' courts) (DJMCs), the professional judges who share the work of the magistrates' court. In 2011, magistrates celebrated their 650 year history. The chapter distinguishes between unpaid, volunteer magistrates (lay justices), who are not usually legally qualified and who sit in twos and threes, for a minimum of 26 half-days per year, from DJMCs, formerly known as stipendiary magistrates, who are professionally qualified and normally sit alone, full-time. Both types are called magistrates and Justices of the Peace. Their jurisdiction is almost identical but, through an accident of history, the bulk of the case load in Inner London is heard by DJMCs while in outer London and the provinces it is heard by lay justices. In this chapter we will learn about:

- lay justices' appointment and selection;
- the effort to secure a representative lay Bench, in terms of politics, race and social class;
- the training, removal and discipline of lay justices;
- district judges (magistrates' courts);
- comparing lay and professional magistrates (DJMCs) and suggestions for a mixed bench; and
- magistrates' clerks.

LAY JUSTICES

In 2011 there were around 26,966 lay justices, 51.1 per cent of whom were women and 8 per cent of whom were non-white (Judiciary website). About 2,000 new justices are appointed annually. They are unpaid volunteers who may claim for loss of earnings and other expenses.

Appointment and selection

They are appointed in the name of the Queen to the Commission of the Peace by the Lord Chancellor (L.C.), following approval by the Lord Chief Justice (L.C.J.). They are selected by local Advisory Committees, which consist mainly of magistrates. Any adult under 65 can apply and it is not necessary to be a British citizen. Details of the conditions and qualities sought are on the DirectGov website. The L.C. ran the first *national* recruitment campaign in 1999.

Politics, social background and race

Whereas the doctrine of judicial independence excludes full-time judges from party politics, this is not the case for magistrates. Many are local councillors. Indeed, L.C.s used to direct Advisory Committees to strive to appoint politically-balanced Benches. In 2003, Lord Falconer L.C. announced that voting patterns would no longer be used as indicators of whether a bench reflected the local community. They have been replaced by indicators of occupational, industrial and social groupings, matched against the census.

The work pattern of the lay magistrate excludes certain groups of the population and favours others. Some cannot spare the time to sit, e.g. those who travel extensively for work, those who are establishing businesses and those whose promotion chances depend on their visible efforts at work. For some, sitting as a magistrate would cause a financial loss (e.g. independent business persons and those who are paid by the hour). Justices' "loss of earnings" allowances are only sufficient to compensate the average to low-paid. Groups who can spare the time to sit are over-represented: retired persons, teachers, top management and housewives with older children. The over-representation of some groups can be exacerbated by the fact that, being readily available, they may sit more often than other magistrates. The L.C. set a maximum of 100 sittings per year.

Class imbalance is a source of continuing concern. The Royal Commission on Justices of the Peace (1948) expressed disappointment that the professions and top management were significantly over-represented on the Bench, with a very low proportion of the waged. Research by Hood (1972) and Baldwin (1976) showed that the imbalance had worsened. It had not improved by 1990 (Henham). Auld L.J. emphasised the value of the lay magistracy in the Criminal Courts Review 2001 but commented that there was "scope for improvement, particularly in the manner of their recruitment, so as to achieve a better reflection, nationally and locally, of the community" (p.98).

Complaints used to be made that there were too few minority magistrates, though by 2012, they reflect the population of England and Wales. In 1987, the L.C. acknowledged that the percentage did not mirror the community but, despite his efforts, 1995 statistics showed no improvement. In 2001, his department and Operation Black Vote launched the magistrates' shadowing scheme, encouraging members of minorities to sit alongside magistrates, in the hope of enhancing recruitment. In October 2003, Lord Falconer L.C. launched a Magistrates National Recruitment Strategy to encourage younger people (over 80 per cent of magistrates are over 50), target ethnic minorities and the disabled, and cut sitting days. The Judicial Appointments Annual Report 2004–05 detailed progress, such as improving advertising, helping advisory committees target local underrepresented groups and engaging employers' groups. (See the archived Department of Constitutional Affairs website.) In 2005, a 20-year-old-Asian was appointed to the Horsham Bench. His youth caused some controversy. In 2004, the DCA published research on "Ethnic minority magistrates' experience of the role and of the court environment". It found that 70 per cent of respondents had wholly favourable initial impressions of their bench and 72 per cent had not encountered racist attitudes in fellow magistrates. See further Darbyshire, 2011, Ch.15.

Training

The L.C. is responsible for magistrates' training and the Judicial College has taken on a "strengthened role" pursuant to the **Courts Act 2003**, following the recommendation of Auld L.J., in the Criminal Courts Review, to enhance consistency and quality. Training is generally provided locally, by the justices' clerk and magistrates' clerks, and organised according to the needs of the individual. After the initial induction training (usually a long weekend course), distance learning, prison visits and a few hours of observing court proceedings, if necessary, the justice may commence sitting, as a "winger". A mentor is appointed for each new justice and the justice will undertake about six mentored sittings in the first year, alongside core training. Training needs are assessed according to whether the justice has achieved prescribed competences and, when they are ready, they will be appraised. They receive consolidation training after about a year. After four or five years they may choose to undertake chairmanship training. Justices appointed to youth and family proceedings courts must also undertake specialist training. Magistrates are offered regular continuation training and ad hoc training as the need arises. They are appraised every three years. Statutory provision for magistrates' training is now provided in the **Courts Act 2003** ss.19–21. Details are on the Magistrates' Association website and on the DirectGov website in a booklet entitled *Serving as a Magistrate*.

Removal, disqualification and discipline

The L.C. has power, under the **Courts Act 2003**, to remove a magistrate. Most are removed because they fail to fulfil the required 26 sittings per year. Justices have been removed for being convicted of a criminal offence, being made bankrupt, refusing to apply laws they disapproved of and personal indiscretions. On reaching 70, they are transferred to the Supplemental List. The L.C. may also transfer any justice on the ground of incapacity (**Courts Act 2003**). Complaints are handled by the Office for Judicial Complaints. Disciplinary action was taken against 49 magistrates in 2011-12. The biggest group of complaints is always about inappropriate behaviour or comments (annual report).

DISTRICT JUDGES (MAGISTRATES' COURTS), FORMERLY KNOWN AS SIPENDIARY MAGISTRATES

Professional magistrates are lawyers who satisfy the judicial appointment eligibility condition on a five year basis, under the **Tribunals Courts and Enforcement Act 2007 s.50**. This means, generally, they must be a barrister or solicitor, although other groups, such as legal executives, can now qualify, because of the 2007 Act. They are appointed by the Queen, after selection by the Judicial Appointments Commission, like other full-time judges. In 2011 there were 137 supported by 143 deputies (Judiciary website). The **Access to Justice Act 1999** created a unified bench of district judges, with jurisdiction throughout England and Wales, renaming stipendiary and metropolitan stipendiary magistrates.

COMPARING LAY JUSTICES AND DISTRICT JUDGES (MAGISTRATES' COURTS) AND SUGGESTIONS FOR A MIXED BENCH

In research reported in *The Role and Appointment of Stipendiary Magistrates* (1995) Seago, Walker and Wall found that:

- very few courts had rules for allocating work to stipendiaries (now DJMCs);
- most were assigned general list cases but they also heard long, complex or highly publicised trials and had a heavier caseload than lay justices; and

- they handled all types of work more speedily; one provincial stipendiary could replace 32 justices and one metropolitan stipendiary could replace 24.

They suggested work could be shifted from the Crown Court: "Consideration could be given to an enhanced jurisdiction (up to two to three years imprisonment) for a trial tribunal consisting of a stipendiary and two lay magistrates" (p.145). In 2000, research by Morgan and Russell: *The Judiciary in the Magistrates' Courts*, for the Home Office and Lord Chancellor's Department, made the following findings:

- Lay justices averaged 41.4 sittings per year, plus a week on training and other duties.
- Stipendiaries' work allocation was the same as Seago et al found.
- Stipendiaries' time was concentrated on "either-way" rather than summary (less serious) cases.
- If their caseloads were identical, they could deal with 30 per cent more appearances than lay justices.
- Stipendiaries showed more command over proceedings; court users had more confidence in them as efficient, consistent, questioning appropriately and giving clear reasons.
- Lawyers admitted to preparing better for stipendiaries.
- Lay justices were less likely to refuse bail or use immediate custodial sentences.
- One stipendiary could replace 30 lay justices.
- Doubling stipendiary numbers would cut down court appearances but increase the prison population.
- The net cost would be about £3 million per year.
- Few members of the public had heard there were different types of magistrate.
- Most thought lay justices would be better at representing the views of the community and sympathising with the defendants' circumstances but that stipendiaries would be better at making decisions on guilt and innocence.

In 2000–01 the Institute for Public Policy Research commissioned a MORI poll on the magistracy and then asked Andrew Sanders to compare the skills and experience which lay and professional magistrates brought to the bench. His 2001 paper, *Community Justice–Modernising the Magistracy in England and Wales* reported that:

- a third of respondents did not know the majority of magistrates were lay people;
- they hugely underestimated the proportion of cases they heard; and
- 42 per cent would be more confident in a mixed panel.

Sanders concluded that the skills of both professional and lay magistrates were needed in deciding complex cases: legal skills to apply the relevant law to the facts and social skills to assess character and judge honesty, as well as more practical managerial and administrative skills. Panel decision-making was preferable to sole decision-making. The Civil Liberties Trust, in its report, *Magistrates' Courts and Public Confidence-a Proposal for Fair and Effective Reform of the Magistracy* also recommended mixed tribunals.

In the Criminal Courts Review 2001, Auld L.J. considered this research and the arguments. He concluded that they both did a good job in their separate ways and should retain the summary jurisdiction but should not routinely sit together. As part of his recommendation for a unified criminal court, which was never implemented, he recommended a mixed tribunal as a new middle tier, to hear either-way cases likely to receive up to a two-year sentence. The Bench would comprise two lay justices and a judge, usually a district judge, or judge alone, if the defendant so chose and the court consented. There was considerable opposition, notably from the legal profession, as this would remove the right to jury trial in the Crown Court for a large number of either-way cases. Because of this and the upheaval necessitated in restructuring the criminal courts, the Government rejected the suggestion, in its 2002 White Paper, *Justice for All*. Nevertheless, it planned to shift more work down into the magistrates' court by another means. The **Criminal Justice Act 2003** s.154 doubles the magistrates' maximum sentencing power to one year's custody for a single offence, though it has not yet been put into effect. Magistrates who were the subject of doctoral research by Herbert were opposed to this change. Many felt they were already being asked to handle cases at the extreme of their ability. See synopsis by Zander at (2003) 153 N.L.J. 689 and full report by A. Herbert, "Mode of Trial and Magistrates' Sentencing Powers" [2003] Crim. L.R. 314.

In 2011, the Ministry of Justice published research by Ipsos MORI, *The Strengths and Skills of the Judiciary in the Magistrates' Courts*. It used interviews, discussion groups and court observation. Their findings were as follows.

- Magistrates were perceived as having a greater connection with the community, being fair, less "case hardened" and more open-minded.
- Some associated a bench of three with "a greater degree of democracy".

- Some noted their cost-effectiveness.
- DJMCs were speedier.
- They were perceived as being more adept at case management, especially by legal advisers and defence solicitors.
- Legal advisers provided more support to magistrates (naturally).
- Prosecutors and defence lawyers said they adjusted their case presentation according to the type of bench.
- There was no consistent approach to work distribution. 30 per cent of DJMC cases were "either-way" whereas 18 per cent of lay magistrates' cases were "either-way". Differences not as significant as perceived.
- DJMCs were more costly per case, because they were salaried, but less costly in either-way cases, when CPS, lawyers' and magistrates' volunteering costs were taken into account.
- Evidence suggested that DJMCs were more likely to impose custody.
- Most respondents supported the extension of magistrates' sentencing powers, under the **2003 Act** especially DJMCs, who pointed to the anomaly of higher sentences being available in the youth court. People highlighted cost savings but justices' clerks were concerned about the increased workload in magistrates' courts and an increase in the prison population as magistrates would impose more custody than Crown Court judges.
- Most interviewees were not in favour of mixed benches.

They concluded:

> "...deployment could be made more effective and...systematic... District Judges could be deployed more exclusively on more difficult or complicated cases...savings could be made...if full advantage was taken of District Judges' legally qualified status, and if they were supported by "court associates" rather than Legal Advisers."

MAGISTRATES' CLERKS

Both lay justices and DJMCs are advised by magistrates' clerks. The chief clerk at each court is called the justices' clerk. The nationwide trend of the last four decades has been to amalgamate Benches under one clerkship. Whereas in the 1970s, there were over 400 justices' clerks, in 2012, there were just 27, all professionally qualified. Justices' clerks and staff used to be selected and appointed by magistrates' courts committees but are now part of Her Majesty's Courts and Tribunals Service.

Of course, since justices' clerks are responsible for several courtrooms, normally at more than one court, they delegate advisory functions to assistants. The staff whose job includes advising magistrates in court are called court clerks or legal advisers, of whom there are over 1,800, and they did not need to be professionally qualified until 2010. Delegated legislation requires that, if not professionally qualified, court clerks should be law graduates or equivalent, or possess a special diploma, or be qualified by five years' experience before 1980. A 1995 survey of court clerks' qualifications showed that under half were professionally qualified barristers or solicitors and the Conservative Government refused to require them to be qualified. This led to the curious situation where, in many provincial courtrooms, the court clerk advising the lay justices was not professionally qualified. More anomalous is the fact that in Inner London, where most cases are heard by district judges, most clerks have been professionally qualified for decades, hence the 2011 MoJ research above. In 1999, the L.C.'s Department responded to these criticisms and introduced delegated legislation requiring all clerks to be lawyers by 2010 but exempted the over-40s and those in office before 1998, meaning that there are many advisers in these groups who are not professionally qualified lawyers.

Revision Checklist

You should understand:

- **the significance of magistrates in the English legal system and the work of their courts;**
- **the difference between lay justices and district judges (magistrates' courts) and what research has shown about the differences in the way they work;**
- **the systems of selecting, appointing and training magistrates and the problems of securing a Bench that represents the population; and**
- **the role of magistrates' clerks (legal advisers).**

FURTHER READING/UPDATING

Darbyshire on the English Legal System (2011), Chapter 15, references therein and website updates

Justice of the Peace; *The Magistrate*, both on *Westlaw*.

websites
DirectGov
Judiciary (statistics)
Magistrates' Association
Ministry of Justice

QUESTION AND ANSWER

The Question

Lord Chancellors have sometimes boasted that magistrates represent a cross-section of society. To what extent is this true? Explain the attempts that have been made to achieve this.

Advice and the Answer

Advice

Do not forget that magistrates include DJMCs, as well as lay magistrates.

Answer guide

1. Briefly consider why Lord Chancellors often say this. This is more of an aspiration than a statement of truth, because magistrates are meant to represent lay people, judging and sentencing their fellow humans in the majority of criminal cases. Symbolically, their abstract and concrete representativeness of the population is very important, then. L.C.s often say "cross-section" or "representative" in morale-boosting speeches to the Magistrates' Association so look for the latest L.C.'s speech on the Ministry of Justice website. (The L.C. is also the Justice Minister.)
2. Cite the statistics on magistrates on the Judiciary website and compare them with the adult population of England and Wales in the last census (Office for National Statistics is the official, free, government website).
3. Consider whether lay magistrates are representative of both genders. Clearly they are almost perfectly representative and much more so than professional magistrates, DJMCs, whose statistics are also on the judiciary website.
4. Do they represent the ethnic breakdown of E & W?

5. Do they represent adult age distribution in E & W? Almost certainly not, since over 80 per cent of them are over 50. Why is that and why is it undesirable?
6. Do they represent a social distribution? You cannot answer this from the official statistics but look at the points made above. Certain groups are over-represented and it is very difficult to attract other groups. Why?
7. Consider my important point above, that even if a representative lay bench could be constructed, the people who can spare more time sit more often than others. You might speak to the magistrates' clerks (legal advisers) of your local magistrates' court to ask whether some magistrates sit more than others and you can go and visit your local court frequently and see for yourself what the bench looks like. Does it appear to represent the local population, or do you expect to see a predominance of white, white-haired females?
8. Are professional DJMCs more or less representative? They are younger but, by definition, they are all middle class, because they are all lawyers.
9. Why does the L.C. want to attract a more diverse bench? Back to the legitimacy point again (1).
10. What steps has he taken to try to recruit a more balanced bench? Consider whether it will ever be possible or desirable to recruit a cross-section of the population. People with criminal records are excluded, as are people with insufficient command of the English language. They are excluded from juries too. Look at the magistrates' selection criteria on the DirectGov website. What groups does that exclude? Most people have no idea who magistrates are or what they do, let alone that any adult can apply to be one. Can you think of other ways to attract under-represented groups? Even if every member of the adult population knew they could apply, could they be bothered to be a magistrate? Can you think of anything to attract them?

The Jury

INTRODUCTION

Juries mainly sit in the Crown Court where, if the defendant pleads not guilty, he has to be tried by a judge sitting with 12 jurors. The judge decides points of law, conducts the trial and does the sentencing, and the jury brings in the verdict of guilt or innocence on the evidence. Juries are also used in coroners' courts and, rarely, in the civil courts. This Chapter examines eligibility for jury service and the arguments surrounding the jury.

ELIGIBILITY

This is laid down in the Juries Act 1974, as amended by the **Criminal Justice Act 2003**. Those qualified are people on the electoral register, aged 18–70, who have lived in the UK for five years since the age of 13. The Act does not stipulate random selection. The Act included long lists of the disqualified, the ineligible and the "excusable as of right". This, along with discretionary excusal by the court, destroyed randomness and was criticised by Auld L.J. in the *Criminal Courts Review*, Ch.5 (background research in Darbyshire et al, "What can the English Legal System learn from jury research published up to 2001?").

KEY POINT

Auld L.J. recommended that everyone should be qualified for jury service, except the mentally ill. This was accepted by the Government and was enacted in Sch.33 to the **Criminal Justice Act 2003**. This was controversial, since doctors, nurses, lawyers, judges and criminal justice professionals may now be summoned. Only serving members of the armed forces have a right to excusal, if certified by their commanding officer.

He recommended that the category of the *disqualified* should not change. Consequently, the 2003 Act preserves the disqualification of people on bail, people who have ever been sentenced to custody or alternatives for five years, or who, in the last ten years, have been so sentenced.

Selection from the electoral roll

This is done randomly. The roll is problematic. It is not accurate, because of population mobility, house moves, death, and people not registering, especially to evade council tax. Auld L.J. recommended that, as in the US, the roll should be supplemented by other publicly maintained lists or directories. (For background, see the paper by Darbyshire et al, above). The Government rejected this recommendation.

Discretionary excusal

Section 9 (2) of the **1974 Act** permitted further inroads into randomness by allowing jury summoning officers to accept excuses for good reasons. Acceptable excuses were highly subjective.

KEY POINT

In 2000, the Jury Central Summoning Bureau (JCSB) was introduced, administering a nationwide and supposedly consistent summoning and excusal system, following a 1999 Home Office survey by Airs and Shaw exposing widespread and inconsistent excusals.

Despite the new scheme, however, Darbyshire et al reported, in 2001, that the Bureau had found that a very large proportion of those summoned ignored their summonses and were not pursued by the court. Auld L.J. recommended prohibiting easy excusals. Consequently, the **Criminal Justice Act 2003** places a duty on the Lord Chancellor (L.C.) to issue guidelines and this was done in 2003. Since 2004, only those who can prove that they cannot not *defer* service are excused. Compelling reasons for deferral include a pre-booked holiday or death or illness of a close relative. Compelling reasons for *excusal* include insufficient understanding of English, certain care responsibilities and religious beliefs that are incompatible with jury service. In the press release announcing this stricter line on excusals, the Government claimed that the **2003 Act** would double the number of those eligible for jury service. As judges and lawyers can now be summoned for jury service, lawyers' professional bodies and the Lord Chief Justice (L.C.J.) issued guidance on when they should ask for a transfer to a different court.

The law lords heard three test cases on these provisions of the 2003 Act. The appellants claimed that the inclusion of police officers and a Crown Prosecution Service lawyer prejudiced the fairness of their trials, in *R. v Abdroikov and joined cases* [2007[UKHL 37. The law lords upheld their claims of bias. Justice had not been seen to be done. Dissenting, Lord Roger said the judgment drove a coach and horses through the 2003 Act. Zander called this a "troublesome decision": (2007) 157 N.L.J. 1530. In *Hanif and Khan v the UK* (ECtHR, 20 Dec 2011; [2012] Crim. L.R. 295), one juror was a police officer. He knew a police officer, a prosecution witness. They had worked together in the past. The judge allowed the juror to continue, with a warning about impartiality. The ECtHR found that art.6 was violated. A judicial warning was insufficient to guard against the risk that the juror might, albeit subconsciously, favour the police evidence. A tribunal must be *objectively* as well as *subjectively* impartial. The court surveyed many common law and other jurisdictions. The overwhelming majority made police officers *in*eligible to serve on juries. A number of law reform commissions had considered the issue since 2003. Scotland, Ireland, New South Wales and Western Australia had decided not to follow the English change. The ECtHR had not been asked to decide whether the **2003 Act** breached the **Convention**. See P. Hungerford-Welch, "Police Officers as Jurors" [2012] Crim. L.R. 320.

Excusal by the judge

Under the **Juries Act 1974** s.10, the judge may discharge from service any juror about whom there is doubt as to "his capacity to act effectively as a juror" because of physical disability or insufficient understanding of English. Additionally, judges have a common law discretion to discharge jurors—for instance those who have any connection with the parties. People who have been denied excusal by the JCSB regularly ask judges if they can be excused, by writing letters or asking in the courtroom. There has been no research as to how judges exercise this discretion. In 2006, a new version of the **Consolidated Criminal Practice Direction** was issued (HMCTS website). Guidance to judges appears at para.IV.42.1. It is very vague: "Such applications must be considered with common sense and according to the interests of justice".

Removing jurors from a jury

The group attending a particular Crown Court, from which juries are selected during a two-week period, is called "the panel". There are a number of ways in which any one of them can be removed from a specific jury.

Vetting

Checks may be made against the names of the jurors on the panel in certain instances. The Attorney General's (Att Gen's) 1980 guidelines distinguish between (a) vetting carried out by the police and (b) "authorised checks", requiring his personal consent.

- Police may make checks against criminal records, following guidelines set down by the Association of Chief Police Officers, to establish that jurors are not disqualified.
- "Authorised checks" are very rare and take place in trials involving national security, such as terrorist trials, and those of offences under the **Official Secrets Act 1989**. They are carried out only with the Att Gen's permission, following a recommendation by the Director of Public Prosecutions. The DPP decides what part of the information disclosed should be forwarded to the prosecution, *not* the defence.
- In cases falling under the guidelines, after an "authorised check", the Att Gen will consider, and in other cases the Chief Constable may consider, defence requests for information revealed on jurors.

Challenges to the array

Once the panel has been assembled, all parties have a common law right, preserved by s.12 (6) of the **Juries Act 1974**, to challenge the whole panel on the grounds that the summoning officer is biased or has acted improperly, e.g. this was attempted in *Danvers* [1982] Crim. L.R. 680 by a black defendant, on the grounds that the all-white jury did not reflect the ethnic composition of the community.

Challenge by the prosecution

The prosecution may exclude any panel member from a particular jury by asking them to "stand by for the Crown" without reasons, until the whole panel, except for the last 12, is exhausted. Reasons ("cause") must be given for any further challenges but, with panels often consisting of 100 or more, the prosecution rarely needs to explain its challenges. The Att Gen announced, in 1988, that this prosecution right would be limited to two instances: to remove a "manifestly unsuitable" juror; or one in a terrorist or security trial where the Att Gen has authorised vetting.

Challenges by the defence

Once the jury are assembled, the defence may challenge any number for cause (good reason acceptable to the judge), but what is an acceptable "cause" was qualified by a 1973 **Practice Note** issued by the Lord Chief Justice, who stated it was contrary to established practice for jurors to be excused on grounds such as race, religion, political beliefs or occupation.

Until 1988, the defence could make a number of *peremptory* challenges, without reasons. This was abolished, amidst great controversy, by the

Criminal Justice Act 1988. This resulted from unsupported allegations that the right was being abused by defence lawyers and the recommendation of the *Roskill Committee on Fraud Trials* 1986 that it be abolished. This leaves a gross imbalance between prosecution and defence rights but, although challenges were controversial in the 1980s, the argument has died down because they are rarely used by either side. In this respect, English and Welsh courts are the opposite of American ones.

Race

Auld L.J. considered the research paper by Darbyshire et al, which concluded that the preponderance of research, worldwide, suggested that jury verdicts were affected by the racial composition of the jury. Like the **Royal Commission on Criminal Justice 1993**, he recommended, in 2001, that in a case where race was relevant, a scheme should be devised for selecting up to three ethnic minority jurors. The Government rejected this (*Justice for All*, 2002). In *R. v Smith (Lance Percival)* [2003] EWCA Crim 283, the CA affirmed that a jury may not be racially constructed.

In 2007, the Ministry of Justice published research by Thomas, *Diversity and Fairness in the Jury System.* She found "there was no significant under-representation of minority groups among those summoned at virtually all" Crown Courts (p.i), although some groups were underrepresented in some courts, because of inadequate command of English "Almost half of all Pakistani jurors summoned did not serve" (p. 95). See critique by Darbyshire at [2008] Crim. L.R. 888 and reply by Thomas at 891. In 2010 the Ministry published very important results of a large-scale project by Thomas in *Are Juries Fair?* The study found that verdicts of all-white jurors did not discriminate against BME defendants. It confirmed that BME defendants were more likely to plead not-guilty than whites. There was a 63 per cent conviction rate for white and Asian defendants and a 67 per cent conviction rate for blacks. This strongly suggested that racially balanced juries were unnecessary for fairness but there were concerns about appearances of fairness with all-white juries, especially at courts with many BME defendants.

CONTROVERSIES SURROUNDING THE JURY

There is a debate between civil libertarians and others about the pros and cons of retaining the jury, and jury equity.

Should the jury be retained and does it inject layman's "equity" into the legal system?

Pro

1. The jury rouses strong emotions and is defended as a "constitutional right" and a guardian of civil liberties. Devlin hailed it as a guardian of democracy, "the lamp that shows that freedom lives" (*Trial by Jury*, Hamlyn, 1956) and Blackstone called the jury "the glory of English law" (*Commentaries on the Laws of England*, Vol. IV, 1768). It is argued that it acts as a check on officialdom, on the judge's power, and as a protector against unjust or oppressive prosecution, applying jury "equity" — deciding guilt or innocence according to a non-lawyer's feeling of justice rather than by applying law to facts proven beyond reasonable doubt. In *R. v Wang* [2005] UKHL 9, the HL held that there were no circumstances in which a judge could direct a jury to convict, though the CA qualified this in *R. v Caley-Knowles* [2006] EWCA Crim 1611.
2. Jury trial is argued to be fairer than trial by judge alone, since it is likely that 12 people will cancel out one another's prejudices.
3. A decision by representative members of the community confers legitimacy on the verdict. People are more likely to accept it than a judge's verdict.

Con

1. The importance of the jury system is overrated. When given the choice, most defendants choose to appear before magistrates (source: annual *Criminal Statistics*, Home Office website) and, of the remainder who opt for the Crown Court, about three-quarters plead guilty and thus are not tried by jury but just sentenced by the judge. Thanks to this and the downgrading of offences, only around one per cent of defendants are now tried by jury (Darbyshire, 1991).
2. Use of civil juries has declined since the nineteenth century. The Administration of Justice (Miscellaneous Provisions) Act 1933 imposed limits on the use of civil jury trial, which remains available only in cases of libel, slander, malicious prosecution, false imprisonment and fraud, but the court can refuse it. (If enacted, the Defamation Bill 2012 will remove the *presumption* that defamation cases will be tried by jury). Examining the reasons why people do not opt for civil juries gives an idea of the drawbacks of jury trial. For example, the Faulks Committee 1974 recommended jury trial should no longer be available as of right in defamation actions for these reasons:

- Judges were not as remote from real life as popularly supposed.
- Judges gave reasons; juries did not.
- Juries found complex cases difficult.
- Juries were unpredictable.
- Juries were expensive (jury trial is slower, as explanations have to be geared for them, not a judge).

3. Additional anti-jury arguments are:
   - They do not always take notes, are not encouraged to do so, and may not be able to remember all the evidence, thus they are likely to be swayed by the more dominant characters' interpretation or recollection of events. They are more likely than a judge to be distracted from deciding on the evidence by the appearance and personalities of the witnesses.
   - They have difficulty in understanding evidence in some trials. This is most acute in long and complex fraud trials, discussed below.
   - The notion that the jury applies its own "equity" has no substance. Baldwin & McConville in *Jury Trials* (Clarendon, 1979) found no evidence that juries acquitted people in the face of unjust prosecution. On the contrary, perverse verdicts (contradicting the evidence) occurred at random. The jury thus had the disadvantage of being unpredictable. Auld L.J. considered perverse verdicts at length, in Ch.5 of the *Criminal Courts Review*, and recommended that statute should prescribe that juries had no right to acquit defendants in defiance of the law or disregard of the evidence. Predictably, this provoked widespread opposition from the legal profession, politicians and other interested parties. They pointed out that the ability of a jury to apply its own equity is one of the traditional justifications for its use in determining verdicts in serious crimes. The Government rejected this recommendation.

Fraud Trials

These were considered by the Roskill Committee on Fraud Trials in 1986. Serious and complex fraud trials are notoriously long (often over 100 days), expensive and highly complicated. The Committee recommended the jury be abolished in complex criminal fraud cases and be replaced by a Fraud Trials Tribunal of a judge and two lay members with a knowledge of accountancy and bookkeeping. Calls for the jury's replacement in serious frauds were renewed after the costly Maxwell brothers' trial in 1995–96. In 1998, the Home Office published a consultation paper and in 2000 the Fraud Advisory Panel suggested a number of reforms. In his *Criminal Courts Review* 2001, Auld L.J. recommended empowering trial judges, in serious and complex frauds, to order trial by judge alone. The Government accepted this recommendation. Accordingly, s.43 of the **Criminal Justice Act 2003** *would have* permitted this, under certain conditions.

KEY POINT

Section 43 was very controversial and was not implemented, because it provoked strong opposition. It was repealed in 2012.

Nevertheless, the collapse of the London Underground Jubilee Line extension corruption trial in 2005 because of juror problems, after almost two years and a cost of £60 million, caused fresh calls for non-jury trials in these cases. The Lord Chief Justice said that fraud trials should be reorganised and confined to three months in length and the Attorney General launched a fraud review, reporting in 2006. In 2006, the Home Secretary introduced the **Fraud (Trials without a Jury) Bill,** rather than activating the controversial section above but the bill was predictably defeated, in the Lords, after opposition by the Law Society, the Bar and JUSTICE. The Att Gen continued to be concerned about the declining conviction rate in serious frauds and, in a change of tactic discussed in the 2008 consultation, planned to induce more guilty pleas by offering formal plea bargains. See Chapter 6 on criminal procedure.

Judge-alone trials

In cases of jury "nobbling", Auld L.J. recommended that a judge should be empowered to order trial by judge alone. This was enacted in s.44 of the **2003 Act.** The prosecution can apply for a non-jury trial if there is "evidence of a real and present danger that jury tampering would take place" and that security measures would not prevent tampering. In *T* [2010] EWCA Crim 1035, the CA ruled that the requirements were satisfied in relation to four defendants being tried for armed robbery. The robbery had already resulted in three trials costing £22 million. The third collapsed after a "serious attempt at jury tampering", according to the trial judge. See F. Gibb, "First trial without a jury for 400 years" *Times*, June 19, 2009. They were tried in 2010. See also *G. and others* [2011] EWCA Crim 1338.

Remember that in the magistrates' court, many trials are conducted by a district judge sitting alone. In the US and Canada, the accused can opt for a judge-alone trial and many defendants choose this. For details see Auld's *Review*. He recommended that defendants in England and Wales should have the same choice. The Government tried to introduce it in the 2003 bill but it was defeated in Parliament.

Jury secrecy and impropriety

Juries deliberate in the secrecy of the jury room and disclosure of deliberations is a contempt of court under the **Contempt of Court Act 1981**. This ban includes research which involves questioning jurors on their decision-making. There is also a common law rule, confirmed by the House of Lords, in *Mirza* [2004] UKHL 2 that the court will not investigate or receive evidence about anything said in deliberations, applied in *Smith and Mercieca* [2005] UKHL 12. In 2005, the DCA published a consultation paper, *Jury Research and Impropriety*. This was provoked by a series of cases in which jurors had made allegations of improper behaviour by other jurors, such as racist comments, or relying on information downloaded from the internet. The paper set out the Government's view: research should be confidential and only carried out if permitted by the minister in accordance with a code of conduct, and that the common law should be left as it is. The paper and responses are on the archived Department of Constitutional Affairs website.

In *AG v Fraill and Seward* [2011] EWHC 1629; EWCA Crim 1570 a juror and a defendant were convicted of contempt under the **Contempt of Court Act 1981**, for communicating on Facebook during the trial. See comment at [2012] Crim. L.R. 286. This was a third attempt at a trial. Jurors had been discharged in the two earlier trials. Some Australian jurisdictions have made it a criminal offence for a juror to search online, though this is impossible to police. See editorial "Jurors and the internet" [2011] Crim. L.R. 289, reminding us that C. Thomas found that in high profile cases, 12 per cent of jurors admitted to searching on the internet and 26 per cent said they saw media reports during the trial. A *Times* investigation claimed to have found over 40 examples of public postings that breached the law. These were on open Facebook pages and so were probably far outstripped by what jurors communicate to their friends. They suggested that jurors be warned in writing, not just verbally. For an astonishing case of jurors chatting in the pub with a defendant, see *R. v Hewgill* [2011] EWCA Crim 1778 and the comment at [2012] Crim. L.R. 134.

REVISION CHECKLIST

You should understand:

- **in which courts juries sit and what their function is;**
- **how juries are selected;**
- **who is eligible for jury service;**
- **how and why the Criminal Justice Act 2003 and the creation of the JCSB altered the system of summoning and excusing jurors to respond to concerns over jury composition;**

- how and why jurors can be excluded from serving on particular juries; and
- the arguments raised in controversies surrounding the jury, including the pros and cons of using lay people as decision makers in this way, the debate about removing juries from serious and complex fraud trials and issues about jury secrecy and impropriety.

FURTHER READING/UPDATING

Darbyshire on the ELS (2011), Chapter 16 and material referred to therein and website updates.

Criminal Courts Review, Chapters 5 and 11, National Archives website.

P. Darbyshire, A. Maughan & A. Stewart, *What Can the English Legal System Learn From Jury Research Published up to 2001?* Research for the Criminal Courts Review, Kingston University website.

C. Thomas, *Diversity and Fairness in the Jury System, Ministry of Justice Research Report 02/07* (2007), MoJ website.

Critique of Thomas by Darbyshire and response by Thomas, Crim. L.R. 2008, as referred to above, on *Westlaw*.

P. Devlin, *Trial by Jury* Hamlyn, 1956.

P. Darbyshire, "The Lamp That Shows That Freedom Lives—is it worth the candle?" [1991] Crim. L.R. 740.

Her Majesty's Courts & Tribunals Service website, especially information about jury service, and the **Consolidated Criminal Practice Direction**.

QUESTION AND ANSWER

Question

Outline the arguments for and against jury trial and consider attempts to reduce the use of jury trial.

Advice and the Answer

You need to consider both the material in this chapter and the section of the criminal procedure chapter on mode of trial, because it considers in depth the arguments about the superiority of jury trial and Crown Court trial in general, provoked by attempts to remove the defendant's right to elect jury trial in either-way cases. "Attempts" really include events since the recommendations of the Royal Commission on

Criminal Justice 1993, not the demise of the civil jury in the twentieth century, but you might acknowledge the latter very briefly.

Answer guide

1. List and comment on the arguments in favour of jury trial, starting with Devlin and Blackstone and remembering not to underestimate the very strong attachment the English and Americans have to trial by jury for serious criminal cases, as reflected in lawyers' and politicians' vociferous objections to any attempt to reduce jury trial, described in the "mode of trial" section of the chapter on criminal procedure, and expressed by judges, in cases such as *McIlkenny*, cited in the appeals section of the criminal procedure chapter.
2. In the context of the above, do not forget to mention the obvious arguments, such as safety in numbers, ordinary person's judgment on guilt and innocence, using their collective life experiences, symbolic use of lay people conferring legitimacy on the verdict, making it more acceptable to the defendant and the public, and so on.
3. List and comment on the arguments against.
4. In answering the second part, tell the story of the many recent failed attempts to remove the defendant's right to elect jury trial, told in the criminal procedure chapter.
5. Then add in the sections of the **CJA 2003** described above, permitting the judge to order trial by judge alone but remember that the provision for judge-alone trials in serious and complex frauds was never brought into force, as it was so unpopular.
6. Remember s.13 of the **Domestic Violence, Crime and Victims Act 2004**.
7. You might like to add a brief paragraph on Auld L.J.'s suggestion that the defendant ought to be able to opt for trial by judge alone instead of jury trial. This was included in the **Criminal Justice Bill 2003** but defeated in Parliament.
8. Mention the general point that, apart from 4 to 7 above, there has been progressive reclassification of criminal offences downwards, as explained in the criminal procedure chapter, with indictable offences reclassified as either-way and either-way reclassified as summary offence and, very recently, fixed penalties now commonly imposed for public order offences and minor theft cases such as shoplifting. All of this has resulted in shifting more and more cases out of the Crown Court and thus out of the ambit of jury trial.

Legal Aid

11

INTRODUCTION

Access to Justice

This phrase encompasses, firstly, access to the courts, via cheap and simple procedure, which was the intention of the Woolf Reforms (see Chapter 4) and, secondly, access to affordable legal services, including advice, representation and help with legal problems. Different types of legal aid (LA) have been developed since the mid-twentieth century and some publicly funded help was available before that. Article 6 of the **European Convention on Human Rights 1950** requires that LA should be available where necessary *in the interests of justice* and this principle is about to be adopted by the United Nations. In this chapter we examine the following.

- LA from 2013, under the **Legal Aid, Sentencing and Punishment of Offenders Act 2012 (LASPO).**
- Labour's LA scheme 1999–2013, under the **Access to Justice Act 1999**.
- Why was the pre–1999 scheme inadequate?
- Evaluation of the 1999–2013 scheme.

KEY POINT

A national, statutory scheme of legal aid and advice for civil legal problems was established by the **Legal Aid and Advice Act 1949**, resulting from the Rushcliffe Committee 1944–45. The scheme developed was the judicare model, the provision of services by paying fees from state funds to private practice lawyers. Rushcliffe's second suggestion, of a network of legal advice centres, staffed by fulltime state-salaried lawyers, like NHS doctors, was never implemented. Criminal LA was developed from the 1960s, including duty solicitor schemes in magistrates' courts and police stations. Thirdly, legal advice was developed separately. The three schemes were brought together under the **Legal Aid Act 1988**, which created the Legal Aid Board. In 2007, Sir Henry Brooke, a retired appeal judge, said that most lawyers, like him, used to undertake legal aid work and the legal aid scheme used to be "the envy of the world".

LEGAL AID FROM 2013, UNDER THE LEGAL AID, SENTENCING AND PUNISHMENT OF OFFENDERS ACT (LASPO) 2012

In November 2010, the Coalition government published a consultation called *Proposals for the Reform of Legal Aid in England and Wales*. This explains the policy behind the Act. Explanatory notes accompany the Act on the Legislation website. The Act takes LA back within the Ministry of Justice, administered by an executive agency (s.38). The Legal Services Commission, which ran LA under the **1999 Act**, is abolished (s.38). The Labour Government had already decided to do this, following Ian Magee's proposals in his review of the delivery of LA. The LSC had been criticised. In 2012, it had its accounts qualified for the fourth year running. The National Audit Office noted that it had paid excessive fees of more than £20 million to LA lawyers and £15 million went to recipients who were not eligible for help. Lawyers are critical of the 2012 Act because, instead of LA being available for everything unless specifically excluded, as under the **1999 Act**, we now have the reverse regime: LA is now limited to those matters specified in the Act (Sch.1). I have emphasised key words.

- Section 1 makes the *Lord Chancellor*, Minister of Justice, *responsible for the provision of LA*. This is not new and has been the case since LA was invented.
- Section 4 is novel, creating a *Director of Legal Casework* to decide on LA in individual cases. He must comply with the L.C.'s published directions and follow his guidance. The L.C. must not interfere with individual case decisions and must ensure that the Director acts independently.
- Section 8 *defines civil legal services* as including providing advice and assistance on law, legal proceedings and legal disputes. Services can include representation, mediation and assistance in other dispute resolution. This definition is not new but it is *very important* to the Government that *help with mediation and ADR* are provided for in a *statute*, because, like all governments since 1990, they emphasised the importance of using ADR instead of court proceedings, in order to reduce costs.
- Section 10 allows for LA provision in *exceptional cases*, where required under the **Human Rights Act** or EU law.
- Section 11 requires the L.C., in setting LA criteria, to take account of the *cost benefit* of legal service and resources available. This is important to the Government because, like all their predecessors since the 1980s, they want to cut costs. The L.C. must take account of the applicant's prospects of success (not new), future demands for LA, whether alternatives are available, the importance to the individual, the seriousness

of the issue, the applicant's conduct and the public interest. The criteria *re-emphasise ADR, including mediation.*

- Section 15 allows the L.C. to make regulations about criminal LA. He must have regard to the *interests of justice*. This is required by art.6 of the **European Convention on HR**, drafted by the British. Not surprisingly, it has been the criterion for the grant of criminal LA since the 1960s.
- Section 17 specifies that regulations will determine eligibility according to the applicant's financial resources and the interests of justice. These two tests, *the means test and the merits test* have been applied to all types of criminal and civil LA since LA was invented.
- Section 19 provides for regulations permitting courts to grant LA. Nothing new. Courts were always responsible for granting criminal LA.
- Section 23 allows for rules requiring people to pay a *contribution* towards their LA. Not new.
- Section 25 allows for the *cost* of civil LA to be *recouped from property* recovered or costs secured. Not new. A charge may be placed on a property. When it is ultimately sold, the money owed must be paid back to the LA fund. (Again, not new).
- Section 26 provides that when *costs* are ordered in legally aided civil proceedings, they must be *reasonable*, taking account of the financial resources of all the parties, and their conduct.
- Section 27 says that the L.C. is under no duty to provide the services by a means selected by the applicant. *Services can be provided by telephone or other electronic means*. This is not novel. For instance, a police station detainee will often receive only telephone advice from a duty solicitor or other lawyer in the middle of the night.
- Section 27(4) provides that a *recipient of criminal LA may select* ***any*** *representative* who is authorised to provide criminal LA. This is not new. Free choice of lawyer is required by the **ECHR** art.6. This means that an applicant can never be restricted to representation by a public defender, as is the case in the USA.
- Section 29 requires the L.C. to produce a *code of conduct* for civil servants and LA providers. It must include duties to avoid discrimination, duties to the courts and so on.
- Section 41 gives the L.C., the Minister, 13 new powers to make regulations. Ministers have always had sweeping legislative powers to run LA schemes.
- Schedule 1 lists *the types of civil legal services* that may be provided for, such as care, protection and supervision of children, special educational needs, child abuse, mental health and incapacity, community care, facilities for the disabled, appeals about benefits, family homes and domestic violence, family mediation, forced marriage, judicial

review, habeas corpus (applications for release by the unlawfully detained), public authority abuse of power, breach of **Convention** rights, the Special Immigration Appeals Commission, immigration, loss of home, ASBOs, services for victims of gang-violence, human trafficking, harassment, inquests, pollution, equality, cross-border disputes, and terrorism prevention, among other services. The novelty here is the inclusion of such a long, detailed list in the Act. Ken Clarke explained that the aim was to stop LA branching out too far, as it did under Labour.

- Schedule 2 lists *excluded* services. Some of these are *uncontroversial* and have always been excluded: defamation, property conveyancing, will-making, trusts, company, partnership and business issues.
- *Very controversially*, Sch.2 excludes a list of services formerly amenable to civil LA: claims for personal injury (first excluded by Labour in 1999, amid furore); claims in the torts of negligence, assault, battery, false imprisonment, breach of statutory duty, and trespass; and property damage cases, state benefits and criminal injuries. Negligence includes clinical negligence, which is *intensely controversial*.
- Critics will be encouraged by the fact that advocacy is provided for in a list of about 20 types of tribunal proceedings. A historic criticism of LA was that it did not provide tribunal representation.

Background: The Coalition Government's Policy Behind the 2012 Act

In 2010, the Coalition replaced Labour. Ken Clarke became Minister of Justice and Lord Chancellor, with a remit to cut the justice budget drastically. The Act replaces the regime established by Labour, under the **Access to Justice Act 1999**. In *Legal Aid: Reforming Advocates' Graduated Fees* (2010), the Government consulted on aligning defence fees with (lower) prosecution fees. This problem of the imbalance between prosecution and defence was identified 20 years ago but lawyers resisted attempts to deal with it.

In 2010, he published the consultation paper mentioned above. He said the LA system was one of the most expensive in the world and bore little resemblance to the scheme introduced in 1949. It covered a very wide range of issues, including some that should not require any legal expertise. There had been 30 consultations since 2006. "I want to discourage people from resorting to lawyers whenever they face a problem, and instead ...consider alternative methods of dispute resolution..." He said he was consulting on the Jackson recommendations on civil procedure (see Chapter 4) and asking David Norgrove to reform family procedure, and he had been working with the Home Secretary and the Attorney General to transform criminal procedure. Here, I summarise the main points and add comments in square brackets.

- These proposals would cut LA costs by **£350 million**.
- Chapter 2: In the criminal process, they planned to **cut bureaucracy**, improve communication between agencies and emphasise **case management**. They would offer **sentence discounts** to encourage the earliest possible guilty pleas. [He suggested 50 per cent discounts but media outrage caused him to drop this]. **Restructured lawyers' fees** would encourage this. In civil cases, the Jackson review of costs recommended more proportionality, and making success fees and "after the event" insurance irrecoverable.
- Chapter 3: History.
- Chapter 4: **No change in criminal LA**.
- Chapter 5: Proposals for eligibility changes in civil and family LA, including taking account of property equity. **Contributions** from clients' income **should increase**. Everyone with £8,000 disposable capital should contribute, including those on benefits.
- Remuneration: **competitive pricing** should be introduced [deeply unpopular with lawyers but Lord Chancellors have been contemplating it since the 1990s].
- Chapter 7: Proposed **reducing civil and family fees** "across the board" by ten per cent. The use of QCs in family cases should be controlled. They were used in care cases and paid up to £100,000.
- Chapter 8: **Experts' fees** ought to be reduced by ten per cent, moving towards fixed or graduated fees.
- Chapter 9: **Proposed alternative funding sources**—interest from solicitors' client accounts, as in Australia, NZ, USA, S. Africa, Zimbabwe and France; and taking a proportion of legally aided claimants' damages towards a Supplementary LA Scheme, and encouraging legal protection insurance, as recommended by Jackson. [This has been suggested since the 1970s. Research shows that the British have little appetite for it. People insure pets for £12 a month. Only one in seven consumers were prepared to pay £75 per year for legal expenses insurance.]
- Chapter 10 proposed **bringing LA within the MoJ** and reducing bureaucracy, following a recommendation of Ian Magee, commissioned by Labour: *Review of Legal Aid Delivery and Governance*, 2010. [Labour proposed to abolish the LSC after the Parliamentary Public Accounts Committee reported in 2010 that its "lax financial controls" caused it to overpay solicitors £25m in 2008–09.]
- Chapter 4: Set out proposals to **limit the scope of LA** but the power would be retained to grant aid to exceptional cases.
- Target resourcing: the grant of LA depended on the capacity of a person to represent themselves, the type of proceedings, and the complexity of law and evidence. **LA should be the "funder of last resort"**, the

conditional fee agreement (no-win no-fee) being the first resort. Other organisations, e.g. voluntary sector, could provide advice on welfare and housing. The Government had considered other means of dispute resolution, e.g. ombudsmen, complaints procedures.

> "[We] propose a revised civil legal aid scheme which focuses resources on those cases where the litigant is at risk of very serious consequences. Examples include facing the removal of their children, physical harm or homelessness, or where legal aid is justified to ensure a fair society through empowering citizens to hold the state to account or to meet our legal obligations, for example, in relation to reciprocal arrangements on international child abduction."

- The **civil** LA **merits test** would be **retained.**
- The massive annexe lists what was "in scope", what would be retained and removed.
- **"In scope"** would include roughly those issues listed in the Act, above, such as: cases where litigants are incapable of representing themselves, e.g. elderly, frail, disabled, asylum-seekers, immigrants in detention and so on; allegations of abuse; community care; debt where the client's home is at immediate risk; domestic violence; family mediation; housing; mental health; children; inquests, harassment, gang violence injunctions; environmental matters; and EU cross-border litigation. [The withdrawal of LA for family cases except for domestic violence was severely criticised. The definition of domestic violence had to be widened as the Act passed through Parliament.]
- **"Out of scope"**: the existing exclusions; money claims, such as consumer credit, except e.g. damages for child abuse; cases resulting from the litigant's own decision, e.g. immigration; *representation* in inquests and tribunals, generally; and ancillary relief (family property), without violence.

> "We propose to make changes to the courts' powers to enable the Court to redress the balance in cases where one party may be materially disadvantaged, by giving the judge the power to make interim lump sum orders against a party who has the means to fund the costs of representation for the other party. In doing so, the Court would also incentivise the contributing party to negotiate a settlement."

- Also out: **clinical negligence**; criminal injuries; education, employment; housing, e.g. right to buy; welfare benefits; and tort and other general claims. [Excluding clinical negligence from LA will save £17 million per year but has been criticised by the House of Commons Health Committee, who noted that Jackson L.J. said that it was "vital" for LA to be retained in such cases].
- "Out" would be **private law children and family cases.** "Legal aid is encouraging long, drawn-out and acrimonious cases which can have a significant impact on the long-term well-being of any children involved". [All of the new categories classified as out-of-scope caused uproar among lawyers' groups. Predictably, threats to cut back on LA always cause very vociferous protests. Part of this is a genuine concern about the perceived whittling away of access to justice, especially by vulnerable citizens. Part is self interest. Lawyers made a very good living out of LA in the 1980s and 1990s. They expected that this would continue.]
- Public interest cases are currently funded. This should not necessarily bring a case back in scope, in future.
- There should be a **scheme for excluded cases**, to meet our obligations under the **European Convention on Human Rights**. The proposed criteria would be: significant wider public interest; overwhelming importance to the client; or complexity.
- The paper emphasised **telephone advice** "we will provide a simple, straightforward telephone service...the single gateway to civil legal aid services".
- The Government acknowledged the **increase** in numbers of **litigants in person**. Many cases could be resolved out of court. There was no evidence on the impact of a litigant in person on the outcome of proceedings, according to research published by the Department of Constitutional Affairs, in 2005. [The author of this research, Professor Moorhead, claimed that the Ministry was misrepresenting his research. These proposals disturbed judges, at the thought of having to cope with many more unrepresented litigants.]
- Lawyers were paid more for guilty pleas in the Crown Court, plus a committal fee.
- **Fees** should be made more even, in triable-either-way (TEW) cases, and the committal fee should be abolished. [In October 2011, the Government introduced fixed fees for Crown Court cases, where magistrates had determined that the case was suitable for summary trial. This means that, if magistrates think your case is suitable for them to keep, your lawyer will get one fixed fee, even if you chose to go to the Crown Court. This fee will include all hearings. As is obvious, this provides a

massive incentive for the defence to opt for the magistrates' court and, if they choose the Crown Court, for the defendant to plead guilty, to get the case over with, quickly. They also reduced the difference for late and early guilty pleas offered in the Crown Court.]

- Litigators and advocates were **paid according to the number of pages of prosecution evidence.** This should be replaced with a better indicator of complexity.
- Three sets of fees applied in magistrates' courts: rural; urban; and London. The London differential was not justified, given the supply of solicitors.
- Some CPS rates were significantly lower than defence rates, e.g. sentencing hearings were half.
- Fees in very high cost cases should relate to outputs not hours of input.
- In 2008–09, LA payments to QCs and leading junior barristers cost £52 *million*. The average number of prosecution pages had increased by 65 per cent since 2004–05. This reflected the use of mobile phone records.

Criticisms of the 2013 Scheme

In addition to the specific criticisms made in square brackets, above, The Law Society proposed an alternative set of savings at *www.soundoffforjustice.org*. The Family Law Bar Association said there would be a dangerous inequality of arms in domestic violence cases. The alleged victim would be aided; the perpetrator would not. The very obvious flaw in the proposals is that in family cases, people will make false allegations of domestic violence in order to get LA. R. Smith pointed out in 2009 that even at that time when the MoJ was claiming that we spend much more per capita on LA than other countries, that it was exaggerating (159 (2009) N.L.J. 1527). They ignored the research paper for their department by Bowles and Perry examining what the true figures were. (R. Bowles and A. Perry, *An International Comparison of Publicly Funded Legal Services and Justice Systems*, MoJ research series 14/09 (2009)).

In the meantime, the Bar Chairman acknowledged at their 2010 conference that they would need to diversify away from LA work. They were (yet again) exploring the viability of a Contingency Legal Aid Fund. This idea goes back at least as far as the 1980s. The fund would be used for deserving cases that would not otherwise be brought, because of lack of money. Some of the winnings would then be put back into the fund. Bar chairman Peter Lodder QC, summarising the Bar's response, said the proposed LA cuts "will cause irreparable damage" but there was also a danger of creating greater costs to society, especially with the increased burden of self-represented litigants:

Counsel, April 2011. Lord Chief Justice Judge and other judges were very heavily critical of the proposals, not just because they saw them as a denial of access to justice but also because the massive increase of people representing themselves would slow those proceedings, wasting money and court resources, and create big problems for judges. This is a very important point.

Opposition to the Act continues in 2013. The Legal Action Group's director has called it a "misconceived and unjust piece of legislation" and vowed to make it an election issue in 2015. Many think LA will have to be reinstated for family law, because the courts will not be able to cope. Lord Bach called the removal of LA from social welfare law "not just bad but actually wicked". See further J. Robins 162 (2012) N.L.J. 663. The Law Centres Federation is very concerned about the vulnerability of law centre funding, yet again. Law centres receive on average 46 per cent of their funding from LA. Most will go as a result of the withdrawal of LA from social welfare law. See J. Robins, at *www.thejusticegap.com* and 162 (2012) N.L.J. 979.

The Association of HM District Judges deprecated recent plans to close county court counters, except for two hours a day. They pointed out that judges would waste hours of their time correcting documents if self-represented litigants were denied help in completing forms. See R. Chapman at (2012) 162 N.LJ. 637.

LABOUR'S LA SCHEME UNDER THE ACCESS TO JUSTICE ACT 1999–2013

It is important to understand this because much of this scheme is still in place and will not be scrapped in 2013 when the new system commences.

- Civil LA was largely replaced, in 2000, by a new *legal services* scheme, provided for in the **Access to Justice Act 1999**. Criminal LA was replaced by the Criminal Defence Service. Nevertheless, lawyers still referred to these services as "legal aid". Lord Irvine L.C. explained his plans for these schemes in a 1998 White Paper, *Modernising Justice*, which is on the archived DCA website. The **1999 Act** had replaced the Legal Aid Board with the non-governmental Legal Services Commission to manage publicly funded legal services. They could advise the L.C. The *Community Legal Service* administered civil legal services.
- As for criminal defence, initially, the **1999 Act** provided that all LA in magistrates' courts would be free and representation in the Crown Court would be free, with power to means-test the defendant after the case, in appropriate cases. This had to be abandoned as it proved too

expensive. **The Criminal Defence Services Act 2006** re-introduced means testing in criminal LA. People could be required to pay contributions to their LA, as before. The Government established four public defenders' offices. English lawyers have traditionally been hostile to PDs as they consider them insufficiently independent. By 2006, there were only eight such offices. Criminal defence was still normally delivered by solicitors and barristers in private practice. In July 2000, the L.C. announced he would reduce fees for criminal defence lawyers, to reduce the disparity with prosecutors. This was never fully executed, which is why the Minister of Justice is still trying to do this in 2012.

- The introduction of general civil contracting under the **1999 Act** brought a shift in funding of legal services and *this contracting model has remained in place*. Whereas under the pre-2000 LA scheme, any solicitor could apply to give legally-aided services but few non-solicitor agencies could, all providers of legal help since 2000 must now have a legal services contract and from 2001, all criminal defenders have to have a contract. To get this, an advice agency or firm of lawyers must demonstrate that it satisfies the quality criteria. A provider may have different types of legal services contracts. New Labour, like their predecessors and their Coalition successors, were always trying to get the legal profession to agree to competitive tendering, which lawyers still strongly oppose.

KEY POINT

Conditional fee arrangements ("no win no fee" contracts)

Very importantly, and VERY controversially, the **1999 Act** extended "no win no fee" private contracts, designed to serve people who could not obtain civil legal aid, under the Act. CFAs were permitted by the **Courts and Legal Services Act 1990** but widened in scope by the **1999 Act**. Under Pt II, a CFA is defined, in s.58(2) as "an agreement with a person providing advocacy or litigation services which provides for his fee and expenses, or any part of them, to be payable only in specified circumstances". This means a success fee will be paid only if the lawyer wins the case. Labour announced that LA would not be granted in cases suitable for CFAs. This was enormously controversial. Lord Irvine L.C. was fiercely criticised by lawyers. CFAs were prohibited in criminal proceedings and virtually all family proceedings. Section 29 provided that insurance premiums for policies insuring against the risk of losing the case could be recovered in court costs. Crucially, Lord Justice Jackson, in his 2009 report on costs in civil cases (see Chapter 4), identified high success fees and these insurance premiums as perpetuating the high cost of civil cases, because they were included in the legal costs owed to the winner of the case. As is explained in the chapter on civil procedure, these costs are now curtailed by the **2012 Act**.

The background to the Labour system for civil cases

In their 1999 white paper, *Modernising Justice*, Labour announced that law firms and not-for-profit agencies like Citizens' Advice and law centres would be treated just the same. This was a crucial point because it was a departure from the judicare model, in which LA was originally provided exclusively through the medium of private practice solicitors and barristers. In 1999, the Government published a consultation paper detailing how it would develop the Community Legal Service, setting out the following points. I include these points because they were based on research and are still valid.

- People needed basic information and advice on rights and responsibilities, not necessarily to go to court.
- 6,000 professionals (lawyers) and 30,000 volunteers at Law Centres and other advice centres, such as Citizens' Advice, provided this for £250 million per year.
- This was enough money but service was fragmented and uncoordinated.

The Labour paper gave case studies demonstrating how difficult it was for people with certain problems to obtain satisfactory advice. The lack of an effective *referral* network meant people got initial advice and were then sent away, so the new legal services network should include lawyers, advice workers, paralegals with specialist knowledge, e.g. Trading Standards Officers, and volunteers in Citizens Advice, etc. Need for services varied geographically. Funders were uncoordinated. Time was wasted by advice agencies demonstrating the quality of their services to their different funders. Quantifying legal need was difficult. Statistics indicated that unmet need for legal services resulted not from inadequate provision but from "lack of access to appropriate adequate help of adequate quality".

WHY WAS THE PRE-1999 LEGAL AID SCHEME INADEQUATE?

- Throughout the 1990s, both the Conservative Government then New Labour thought something radical had to be done to reform legal services. Why?
- The cost was "spiralling out of control", according to the Conservative,

Lord Mackay L.C., by the mid-1990s. LA was the only demand-led draw on the Treasury. Some years in the 1990s, the cost rose by 20 per cent, despite the fact that *fewer people* were being aided. The **Children Act 1989**, providing separate representation for children, and the development of duty solicitor schemes in police stations and magistrates' courts accelerated the expense. The media became concerned that a few cases cost millions of pounds. In some cases, wealthy defendants were aided.

- *Unmet legal need* had been identified by research in the 1960s and 70s. It means that where someone has a problem which could be remedied by use of the law, that problem remains unsolved through lack of legal help. It was (and is) caused by:

    - perceived high cost of legal fees;
    - fear of lawyers;
    - lawyers' (historic) lack of training and unwillingness to serve poor clients' needs for advice in welfare law;
    - inaccessibility of lawyers' offices to poor or rural clients;
    - creation of new legal rights without the funding to enforce them;
    - people's ignorance that the law could solve their problem; and
    - the fact that the LA scheme omitted certain services, such as representation at most tribunals.

- By 1999 funders were still uncoordinated. LA was designed to deliver legal services through private practice barristers and solicitors so alternative legal services, listed below, received very little of the huge budget and were dependent on a precarious mix of sources, such as charities, local authorities and other government departments.
- Criminal LA was administered unevenly. Research showed that the "Widgery criteria" post-1960s merits test was applied differently between magistrates' courts, and the Audit Commission criticised them eight years running for failing to apply the means test properly. "Fat cat lawyers", as Lord Irvine L.C. called them, were charging the LA Board exorbitant fees. This, by the way, was an *overwhelming problem*, until 2000. Many civil and criminal lawyers made a *very* good living from legal aid in the 1980s and 1990s, at the taxpayers' expense.
- In 1999, Hazel Genn published a survey of how people solved their legal problems: *Paths to Justice*, summarised at (1999) 149 N.L.J. 1756. She found that people were generally extraordinarily ignorant about their legal rights and obligations.

"Alternative" legal services

Because the shortcomings of the LA scheme, identified in the late 1960s, alternatives to LA delivered by private-practice lawyers were developed and still exist.

- *Law Centres* were established in poor areas, from 1973, with a user-friendly shop front image, where employed lawyers and paralegals provided advice and representation on such matters as welfare law and immigration. They have always suffered fragile funding. Those financed by local authorities found they were biting the hand that fed them, when they acted for groups suffering bad public housing. Funding is unpredictable and unreliable. Sometimes they close temporarily.
- Favoured by the Rushcliffe Committee then Thatcher from 1979, *Citizens Advice Bureaux* now use 20,000 volunteers, advising at over 3,500 locations. They are grossly overstretched, as a 2009 *Times* report disclosed.
- Over 800 independent *advice centres*, covering diverse areas, provide advice and sometimes representation, or make referrals. Lawyers provide advice free but need to refer some clients on if substantive help is needed.
- *Pro bono* groups of solicitors and barristers give free services. The Free Representation Unit, a group of Bar students prepared to represent claimants in tribunals, was established in 1972. The Personal Support Unit in the Royal Courts of Justice was established in 2001, to help self-represented litigants. Lord Woolf initiated this in his 1996 *Access to Justice* report. It now operates at Manchester and Cardiff Civil Justice Centres and elsewhere. It depends on donations and on lawyers acting for free: *www.thepsu.org*. See J. Burke, *Counsel*, March 2011, p.30.
- Governments from the 1980s have promoted ways of helping people solve their problems, to save public money:

    - Helping people represent themselves by simplifying procedure (plain English Civil Procedure Rules; see Chapter 4) and providing advice leaflets and websites.
    - Encouraging ADR, the cheaper and quicker resolution of disputes, out of court (see Chapters 4 and 5).
    - Encouraging private legal expenses insurance.
    - Asking government departments to explain their decisions better and provide accessible complaints mechanisms, like ombudsmen.

EVALUATION OF THE 1999–2013 SCHEME

The scheme was quite visionary. Labour had the simple idea of finding out how much money was spent on LA and alternative legal services and working out the level and nature of local legal needs, and how they could best be fulfilled, whether through private-practice lawyers or alternatives, and thus abandoning the *judicare* model. BUT barristers and solicitors in private practice still provided 92 per cent of civil legal services contracts, thus the model of delivery did not change much. The scheme enabled money to be used in a more imaginative manner. Lord Irvine L.C. extended funded representation to more systems of tribunal and to inquests into deaths in custody and this has been preserved. Public interest cases can now be funded, even if they are in categories normally ineligible. Contracts were granted for telephone advice lines and "outreach" work (advice services provided at alternative venues such as doctors' surgeries or libraries). LA contracts covered debt, immigration, welfare benefits, education and housing. More contracts were granted for such innovations as a virtual law centre and community outreach projects for old people, young people, women in rural areas, and so on. Hundreds of courts provided information points. All of this has been kept.

Advice deserts—unmet legal need got worse

By 2003, the new system attracted widespread criticism because the availability of civil LA via solicitors had radically decreased in some areas, without the provision of alternatives. There were *advice deserts*, such as Kent, where there were no solicitors doing funded housing law. In *Geography of Advice* (2004) Citizens Advice reported a "postcode lottery". The Law Society and the Legal Action Group were concerned that the Government had not enhanced access to justice enough to reduce social exclusion, as it had promised. A 2003–04 survey by the Legal Services Research Centre of the Legal Services Commission, *Causes of Action: Civil Law and Social Justice*, by Pleasance and others, found that one third of adults had experienced a civil law problem in the previous 3.5 years. About a million problems a year were left unsolved as people did not understand their basic rights. Socially excluded groups were especially vulnerable. Civil justice problems often occurred in clusters, such as personal injury causing loss of home or income. 15 per cent of those who sought advice did not obtain any, especially over homelessness, rented housing, anti-social neighbours or benefits. The more advisers a person was referred to, the less likely they were to follow up those referrals. The LSC responded by increasing telephone and online advice and establishing more outreach advice clinics in isolated regions and for specific groups.

Poor remuneration

Solicitors and barristers complained of poor remuneration for publicly funded work, resulting in many of them abandoning it. A Law Society survey in 2003 found that 90 per cent of respondent solicitors were dissatisfied with the poor pay, bureaucracy and audits (checks on their work).

The cost remained problematic

The cost of providing free criminal LA meant a reduction in civil LA. When Lord Carter was asked to report on restructuring the remuneration system, in 2005, the cost of criminal LA had risen by 37 per cent in the previous eight years and spending on civil LA had been reduced by 24 per cent. Criminal defence overspent by £60 million in 2002. The cost of "very high cost" criminal cases rose. There were repeated complaints of the amounts paid to QCs ("fat cats") in such cases. Spending on advocates had risen since 1999 by 20 per cent above inflation. In 2009, the LSC said the average cost of a family case had increased 134 per cent over five years. The Blair Government had created 360 new offences between 1997–2004, without any increase in the LA budget. Ultimately, the response was to abandon free criminal LA and reintroduce means testing. By 2004, 80 per cent of the civil budget was absorbed by family cases.

Several reviews were published in 2004 and they made some calls for fundamental reform or restructuring. For example, the Law Society urged that the budgets for civil and criminal aid should be separated and the Government should develop public legal education. Government departments should acknowledge the demands they created on the LA budget. The Parliamentary Constitutional Affairs Select Committee produced two reports in 2003-04. It criticised LA deserts and persistent unmet need, complaining that only the poorest people were served and people of modest means were denied access to justice. Over-specialisation prevented a holistic approach by solicitors. *The Independent Review of the Community Legal Service* said the Community Legal Service lacked an evidence base to demonstrate how it tackled social exclusion. Contracting and quality assurance were unduly bureaucratic. In 2009, the Legal Action Group, LAG, published *The Justice Gap*, to coincide with the 60th anniversary of LA. They argued that LA had fallen short of its original aims and there was "a marked difference between the numbers of cases pursued to enforce rights and the many potential cases that people never take up as they are either not aware of their rights or they decide it is not worth the trouble to take it further—this is 'the justice gap'". For example, they observed county court housing repossession cases, where "traumatised" people were subject to proceedings from their mortgage lenders and making last-minute negotiations, unsure of what was going on and ill-informed.

Labour government response to criticism, 2005–10

After criticism that there were too many suppliers touting for business amongst asylum seekers, it limited suppliers in this field and introduced salaried solicitors and case workers. After consultation in 2005, it announced cuts.

- Eligibility for representation would be cut, in an attempt to encourage early dispute settlement. Eligibility for help (instead) would be increased.
- Family services would be restructured to encourage early out-of-court settlement. Unreasonable conduct would be deterred. Multiple and repeat applications in private law cases would be curbed.
- In clinical disputes (e.g. against hospitals) and actions against the police, the LSC would be expected to take account of whether the applicant had exhausted all complaints mechanisms.
- Restrictions might be introduced on very high cost civil cases.

In 2005, the Labour government acknowledged the crisis in civil advice, caused by a drop in funding of 22 per cent since 1997. The new strategy recognised the need to provide holistic services. It proposed working with local authorities to establish 75 Community Legal Advice Centres (CLACs) and Networks to "provide access to a service which ranges from basic advice to legal representation in the full range of social welfare problems as well as children and family legal problems". Critics commented that CLACs sounded just like Law Centres and wondered why there was a need to establish a new "brand".

REVISION CHECKLIST

You should know and understand the following.

- **the current model under the 2012 Act;**
- **the reasoning behind it and the controversies over cuts;**
- **the 1999 system it replaced and the defects of that system;**
- **repeating themes; and**
- **in outline, the history of LA.**

FURTHER READING/UPDATING

Darbyshire on the ELS, 2011, Chapter 17, further reading therein and website updates
Law Society's *Gazette* (Lexis)
Legal Action (some parts free on the LAG website)
New Law Journal

Websites (the last two are the most useful)

Bar Council
CLS Direct
Law Centres Federation
Law Society and Law Society's Gazette
Legal Action Group
Legal Services Commission

QUESTION AND ANSWER

Question

Explain the current scheme for legal aid and legal services, and its background. Explore the problems and controversies associated with providing publicly funded legal services.

Advice and the Answer

Advice

There is ample information in this chapter and in the material and websites referred to above to answer the question, because all that is really needed is an intelligent and balanced summary of the story above.

Answer guidelines

1. Outline the new statutory scheme under the 2012 Act and the background as explained in the Minister of Justice's consultation paper. His primary aim was cost-cutting.
2. Explain what the Labour scheme had responded to in the 1999 Act—spiralling cost; limitations of prior legal aid scheme.
3. Examine the criticisms of the 1999 scheme and the Labour government's responses, including backtracking on some policies such as the means test for criminal LA.

4. Comment on the good things about the 1999 model that have been preserved. It was designed to open up and expand the range of providers in the not-for-profit sector.
5. Think about and comment on the problem of providing adequate help for people with legal problems. Are some of these problems insoluble? For example, Lord Mackay, Conservative, in the 1990s, also felt like Labour in 1999 and the Coalition now, that we spent a disturbing amount of money on legal services. He also said that costs were "spiralling out of control". Is there an insoluble problem that, like healthcare, there is a bottomless pit of need and no government can afford to satisfy 100 per cent of that need? Also, bear in mind that lawyers will always oppose cuts in LA, because that is the livelihood of many of them. From the 1970s, we saw a massive expansion of the barristers' and solicitors' professions and much of that was fuelled by the growth in LA. Many judges made a prosperous living as lawyers in that period and some barristers drew "fat cat" fees, running into millions.

Handy Hints and Useful Websites

12

ESSAYS

Identify what is required to answer the question

There are likely to be several elements, each of which requires a response. Do not ignore any element, or you may lose substantial marks or fail. Ensure that you have identified what is required of you. It may be fruitful to check with fellow students that you have fully recognised what is needed, though the work that you produce for assessment *must* be entirely your own.

Research

1. Start by reading the relevant chapters in the core course books that your lecturers/tutors have recommended.
2. It is highly unlikely that you will be able to answer a question by using only a textbook. Examine any further reading that appears to be relevant, that your lecturers/tutors have recommended, or that is referred to in your course text.
3. Examine any electronic or hard copy documents referred to or obviously related to the question or issue that you are researching.
4. Examine legal websites and databases, such as those listed below and in the chapters above. You may wish to download documents and save them to your own computer to read on screen rather than printing them out, which is expensive.
5. Do not start with an aimless Google search and do not even think about citing Wikipedia or similar websites in preference to your textbooks. Use a law dictionary or encyclopaedia such as *Halsbury*, which you can access electronically if you are a university student. Thoroughly search the journals in *Westlaw* and *Lexis*, if you have access to these subscriber databases.
6. Note that this subject changes so rapidly that you need to appreciate that the law, the issues and the circumstances may have changed since the sources you are using were published, including this book. The websites listed here will help you to update the information you have. It is worth checking the press releases archived on the relevant websites and the free updates on *Darbyshire on the ELS* (2011) on Sweet & Maxwell's website.

7. Make accurate notes about the sources of your information including an accurate reference so that you can footnote your sources properly and compile your bibliography.
8. If you are working from your own photocopies, printouts or books, then highlighting is much quicker than taking notes.

Content

Address the terms of the question. This is the most crucial part of the assessment. Those grading your work need to see that you have understood the task and taken the correct approach, so do not "write all you know". You will be assessed on your:

- ability to identify the legal and policy issues raised by the question or problem;
- knowledge of relevant law;
- knowledge and understanding of policy issues, where relevant, including proposals for reform and background to the law;
- ability to conduct careful, thorough, relevant and accurate research; and
- insight into and thoughtful approach to the issues.

"Discuss" means more than just describe the law or topic. It means explain the issues surrounding the topic and address them. For instance, if it is a legal change you are asked to discuss, look at the background to the change in the law. If it is a controversial issue you are asked to discuss, look at the "pros and cons" of the plans, as articulated by Government critics and defenders.

"Critically discuss" or "critically evaluate" does not mean you have to say something bad about the topic. The word "criticism" is used in the sense of theatre criticism. You should look at the pros and cons of the issue, citing relevant sources and, if possible, forming your own opinion. Every *Sun* reader has an opinion on elements of the ELS, such as the jury, but you are expected to develop a well-informed opinion.

Structure

Ensure that there is a clear thread of argument running through your essay. Sub-headings may help you to organise the material and will provide "signposts" to the reader. If you form an opinion, make sure that you acknowledge that there may be different opinions on the subject and briefly address those different opinions. Write a straightforward introduction and conclusion. It will be easiest to write the introduction once you have written the body of the essay. Be as brief as possible. Your introduction should be no more than a very short paragraph.

Expression, style and mechanics

Write in a style which is clear and fluent. Use short sentences. The longer your sentences and the more pretentious your language, the more likely you are to get into trouble. Be very concise. Stick to the word limit. This does not require cutting out the substance. You should read through every sentence many times, ensuring that you have expressed yourself in as few words as possible and not repeated yourself. When I read student essays, I can normally show them how to cut a ten-word sentence down to six. Waffle is your enemy. Carefully proof read your work several times to avoid typographical and other technical errors. List the material you have used in a bibliography and footnote your citations, making sure that you do not abuse footnotes by making substantive points that ought to have been made in the text.

Immaculate use of language is an essential tool of the lawyer's trade

Use of grammar and punctuation affects the meaning of the law and the meaning and quality of your work. Clumsily expressed work with bad grammar and spelling mistakes detracts enormously from the substance of what you are saying. Use a dictionary or a thesaurus but do not forget that the spellchecker on your computer must be set to English (UK). If possible, ask someone to read through your work.

Mistakes of English commonly found in law students' essays

1. Do not use slang and elisions (don't, won't, can't, etc.). You must write in formal English.
2. Capitals: pay attention to your textbooks to find out what words need to begin with a capital. For instance, Parliament and the present Government begin with a capital but not when referring to governments in general. There is one single High Court and one Crown Court but many magistrates' courts and county courts. Nouns in general do not need a capital but titles do.
3. Sentence structure: students commonly use clauses as sentences. Sentences always contain a subject and a verb.
4. "However" is not a conjunction. It cannot be used in a place where "and", "but" or "so" can be used. It should not appear at the beginning of a sentence. Shift it into the sentence and place a comma either side, e.g. "The Government, however, decided not to follow this recommendation".

5. The Grocer's "s": "Cabbage's on special offer today". In this sentence, "cabbages" does not need an apostrophe "s". The word is the plural of "cabbage". "The judge's robes" is a phrase requiring an apostrophe "s" to represent the possessive case and means "the robes of the judge".
6. Paragraphing: choose one type of paragraph break, either an indentation or a line space. Do not mix the two.

Help with English

Around half of first year undergraduates produce essays demonstrating weak use of English, especially those educated in England. Immaculate use of English is not only essential for obtaining a good grade in undergraduate assessments, it is also an essential transferable skill. Learning English is a lifelong task for all of us, including those of us who write professionally. These guides may help. Check for the latest edition.

J. Clancy, *How to Write Essays*
J. Cochrane and J. Humphrys, *Between You and I: A Little Book of Bad English*
D. Collinson, *Plain English*
R.R. Jordan, *Academic Writing*
R. Lawrence, *The Penguin Guide to Punctuation*
G. Leech, *An A–Z of English Grammar*
R. Marius, *A Writer's Companion*
A. Northedge, *The Good Study Guide*
R. Palmer, *Write in Style*
J. Peck, *The Student's Guide to Writing*
M. Swan, *Practical English Usage*
M. Swan, *How English Works*
R. Task, *Penguin Guide to Punctuation*
J. Trezrciak & S. Mackay, *Study Skills for Academic Writing*
L. Truss, *Eats, Shoots and Leaves: the Zero Tolerance Approach to Punctuation*
M. Vince, *Advanced Language Practice*
D. Watson, *Advanced Vocabulary in Context*

Dyslexia

If you are dyslexic, or think you may be, seek out the help of the dyslexia unit at your university. Remember to ensure that lecturers or tutors marking your work know that you are dyslexic.

Plagiarism

Plagiarism is a form of cheating. It means copying someone else's work or ideas and passing them off as your own. If you join with a friend in preparing coursework, make sure the end product is all your own. Do not copy from one another. You may use a large number of sources, such as books, articles and websites, but all must be meticulously cited. You will frequently use secondary sources, such as textbooks. Again, you must point this out. For instance, if you find a useful article or book, quoted in a textbook or another article, then footnote it as "*Fletcher, Rethinking Criminal Law*, as cited in Smith and Hogan's *Criminal Law*, at p.103".

EXAM CHECKLIST

Revision: how?

Start early, otherwise you may waste the summer (or all next year!) revising for a resit. Draw up a revision timetable and stick to it. You will underestimate the time taken to revise. If your lecture notes and others are scrappy, you may find it helpful to make revision notes. Visit the Memory section of the BBC website for a programme containing tips on how to improve your memory *http://www.bbc.co.uk/radio4/memory/*

Revision: what?

1. You should aim to know your whole course fairly well and as much of it as possible in greater depth. Question spotting is very difficult in ELS, as there can be so many different permutations of topics, e.g. "the adversarial process" includes civil and criminal trial and pre-trial; legal profession might be combined with judiciary or with legal services, etc. It helps, however, to know your own course. Know the topics your course teachers have emphasised in your year. Topicality means past papers are, in some respects, unhelpful. Do not revise from notes for other courses and do not fool yourself that this *Nutshell* is anything but a revision aid, a comforter. It is not a substitute for having worked hard and read widely, throughout the year. Beware that it may omit things emphasised in your course, e.g. police powers.
2. Know the approach of your course, as well as its content. Most ELS courses are analytical and discursive, much more so than this *Nutshell*, but the ability to appreciate ELS in the context of this approach comes from wide reading. ELS for undergraduates in non-law courses and students on other courses is usually much more factual, and takes a "tools for the trade" approach.

3. This is the most fast changing area of law. Have you made sure that the information you have been revising is totally up to date? This book was proof read in autumn 2012. Have things changed since then?
4. Have you familiarised yourself with critiques of various elements of the system? Look out for those which have appeared since October 2012. Especially good sources of brief, pithy articles and editorials are the *New Law Journal* and *Legal Action*. Do not forget *The Times* law reports are another great source of brand new case law.
5. Read all the newest consultation papers on the MoJ website and find out what the responses were and whether there were any outcomes in changes of law or practice.

In the exam

Organise your time

Every year I groan over a handful of 2A students who achieve thirds or fails because they have answered two and a half or three questions instead of four. Think about it. If you answer three instead of four, you must achieve an average of 66 per cent in those three, just to attain an examination mark of 50 per cent (just a 2B). Divide the exam time by the number of answers required and force yourself to move on when time is up. Leave ample space between answers to add points, even in neat note form, to your earlier answers, if you can spare ten minutes at the end. Lecturers always say, and some students never seem to understand the simple point, that it is much easier to gain 30 marks on answering a new question than to add 30 to a near-complete one. Do not waffle. Write clearly. Try rollerball or superior ballpoint. See which is quicker and neater. Fountain pens are too slow. Bad writing is bound to affect the markers, as they cannot get the "gist", the "flow" of an argument, even if they can slowly interpret it, word by word. If English is not your first language, practise it by getting as much of your written English checked as you can persuade people to mark (on any topic). Again, if you need remedial help, your college may provide it. In the exam, you need time for mental translation. Time will be your enemy so make every word count. Waffle is even more dangerous for you than for a native student.

Answer the question set

If you panic and misread a question on juries as one on magistrates, you may get 0%. If you "write all you know" where a critical analysis or a particular approach is needed, you may just scrape a pass, if you are lucky. Plan and present your answer and only include that which is required. Do not be tempted to demonstrate knowledge just because you have revised it.

Be authoritative

The trouble with this subject is that every *Sun* reader has an opinion on the jury or the legal profession. You must substantiate your beliefs with fact and authoritative opinion. Most opinions have found written expression in some text, article or committee report, sometimes in many, but do not invent sources/quotations. Your examiner will know better. Being authoritative comes from wide reading, not a *Nutshell*. Be original: very difficult but the more so the better. Reach your own informed opinions. Draw on your own observation of courts and tribunals. They provide hours of free entertainment on a wet Wednesday afternoon. Read a quality newspaper daily. Search for new commentaries and articles in law journals.

ENGLISH LEGAL SYSTEM WEBSITES

Administrative Justice & Tribunals Council *http://ajtc.justice.gov.uk/*
Attorney General *http://www.attorneygeneral.gov.uk/*
Bar Council *www.barcouncil.org.uk*
British and Irish Legal Information Institute *http://www.bailii.org/*
Centre for Effective Dispute Resolution (ADR) *http://www.cedr.co.uk/*
Criminal Cases Review Commission *http://www.justice.gov.uk/about/criminal-cases-review-commission*
Criminal Courts Review 2001, national archives *http://webarchive.nationalarchives.gov.uk/+/http:/www.criminal-courts-review.org.uk/*
Crown Prosecution Service *www.cps.gov.uk*
Department of Constitutional Affairs (predecessor, Ministry of Justice), national archives
http://webarchive.nationalarchives.gov.uk//http:/www.dca.gov.uk/*
European Court of Human Rights *http://www.echr.coe.int/echr*
EC and EU institutions and EC documents, including European Commission and European Court of Justice *http://europa.eu/*
European Commission Representation in the UK, for EU news, publications, info and free email newsletter *http://ec.europa.eu/unitedkingdom/*
UK Government information *http://www.direct.gov.uk/Homepage/fs/en*
Her Majesty's Courts & Tribunals Service *http://www.justice.gov.uk/about/hmcts/*
Home Office *www.homeoffice.gov.uk*

International Courts of Justice are best accessed via the UN website *http://www.un.org/*
Judiciary *http://www.judiciary.gov.uk/*
Judicial Appointments Commission *http://jac.judiciary.gov.uk/*
Judicial College *http://www.judiciary.gov.uk/training-support/judicial-college*
Judicial Committee of the Privy Council *http://www.jcpc.gov.uk/*
Law Commission *http://lawcommission.justice.gov.uk/*
Law Society *http://www.lawsociety.org.uk*
Law Society's *Gazette*: *http://www.lawgazette.co.uk/home.law*
Legal Abbreviations, contains 12,500 abbreviations *http://www.legalabbrevs.cardiff.ac.uk/*
Legal Action Group *www.lag.org.uk*
Legal Services Commission *www.legalservices.gov.uk*
Legislation *http://www.legislation.gov.uk/*
Lexis is a very comprehensive database. Access it via your library's e-resources.
Liberty *www.liberty-human-rights.org.uk*
Ministry of Justice *http://www.justice.gov.uk/*
National Assembly for Wales *http://www.assemblywales.org/index.htm*
Parliament *www.parliament.uk*
Scottish Parliament: *www.scottish.parliament.uk*
The Times http://www.timesonline.co.uk
UK Newsstand, all UK newspapers is available via your library's e-resources.
UK Supreme Court *http://www.supremecourt.gov.uk/index.html*
US Supreme Court *www.supremecourtus.gov*
Westlaw, another very comprehensive subscriber database, containing all case law, statute law many law journals and accessed via library e-resources.

Index

LEGAL TAXONOMY
FROM SWEET & MAXWELL

This index has been prepared using Sweet and Maxwell's Legal Taxonomy. Main index entries conform to keywords provided by the Legal Taxonomy except where references to specific documents or non-standard terms (denoted by quotation marks) have been included. These keywords provide a means of identifying similar concepts in other Sweet and Maxwell publications and on-line services to which keywords from the Legal Taxonomy have been applied. Readers may find some differences between terms used in the text and those which appear in the index.

(all references are to page number)